The Crone

ALSO BY BARBARA G. WALKER

The Woman's Encyclopedia of Myths and Secrets
The Secrets of the Tarot: Origins, History, and Symbolism
The Barbara Walker Tarot Deck

THE CRONE

Woman of Age, Wisdom, and Power

BARBARA G. WALKER

1817

Harper & Row, Publishers, San Francisco

Cambridge, Hagerstown, New York, Philadelphia
London, Mexico City, São Paulo, Singapore, Sydney

FIRST EDITION

Designed by Don Hatch

Library of Congress Cataloging-in-Publication Data

Walker, Barbara G.
    The crone: woman of age, wisdom, and power.

    1. Women—Religious life.   2. Matriarchy—Religious
aspects.   3. Patriarchy—Religious aspects.   I. Title
BL625.7.W35   1985   291.1'78344   85-42939
ISBN 0-06-250928-4

---

85 86 87 88 89 HC 10 9 8 7 6 5 4 3 2 1

Contents

1

Studying the Crone

1

All over the modern world, a new social phenomenon is gradually taking shape. Women, the traditional pillars of Judeo-Christian religion, are turning against this faith. Many women prefer to gather in small grass-roots groups in each other's homes, where they discuss recent studies of prepatriarchal Goddess worship and engage in rituals aimed at recreating some feeling for those ancient faiths.

Because of its private nature, the phenomenon is almost invisible to the public eye. Occasionally, the popular press takes a passing interest in it, giving it the label "witchcraft," which is understood to be mildly newsworthy. Under another one of its labels, "the women's spirituality movement," the phenomenon is hardly defined or even definable in this man's world.

The women's spirituality movement has given many women better feelings about themselves, in consequence of joining together with other women in groups, gatherings, circles, covens, or conferences. Women touch, embrace, communicate. They share food, feelings, thoughts, and ideas. They praise each other's accomplishments. They support each other in trouble. They provide sympathy for hurts, advice for problems, many kinds of mutual education. They laugh or cry together, love or quarrel, lend things, give gifts, do favors. Some find in women's groups the closest relationships of their lives, closer than their bonds with husbands, children, or parents. Others drop out after a time, but with changed attitudes.

Women have always banded together along the underside of male-dominated social structures. Aside from obvious natural bonds among female family members, women have always joined all-female groups that in some way served the mutual support functions listed above, whenever they could. Old-fashioned sewing circles and quilting bees gave their members more than needlework expertise. Grandma's Saturday afternoon teas or Sunday luncheons held more rewards for Grandma and her friends than men ever noticed. Volunteer groups, community services, neighborhood committees, social clubs, church and charity organizations, even bridge clubs or the PTA gave women opportunities to meet and work with one another, to communicate, cooperate, and widen their circles of friends.

Women working together on almost any kind of project have inevitably formed mutually supportive relationships out of their common needs and shared life experiences. When a woman has faced any of life's common crises—birth, bereavement, illness, sudden misfortune, troubles with love or work—there have usually been other women there to help.

Male-dominated society still exploits women's natural propensity to care, to nurture, to take responsibility for the comfort of others. Unfortunately, feminists still allow this to happen. Nothing much has been changed so far by women talking together of the Goddess's blessings instead of the annual fund-raising party, or of the archetypal power of femaleness instead of their children's grades.

As far as most men are concerned, women's talk is still women's talk, having little to do with the "real" world—that is, the world where money is made. Men with power in that world seldom pay attention to what women say among themselves. They even pride themselves on their ignorance of it. They still believe women's groups perform busywork, the only real purpose of which is to keep women off the streets and away from the seats of genuine power.

Because Goddess worshipers use the term *power* much more loosely, they need to understand that, to men, it means the capacity to threaten or destroy. Like it or not, the fate of all women, their children, and their earth lies in the untrustworthy hands of men corrupted by their lifelong craving for that "real" power, which also corrupts women in ways so numerous and so subtle that it takes a very high degree of consciousness-raising to name and avoid even a fraction of them.

Patriarchal society has always found ways to exploit women's need for what is called busywork. Done in solitude, such work has been thought to provide a harmless outlet for frustrated female creativity that will never become commercially viable (the only raison d'être recognizable by the patriarchy). Done in company, such work has been thought to provide harmless ways for women to help one another support male-headed institutions: family, government, church.

A prime example of such exploitation is the churches' canny enlistment of women to work without pay for their cause: promoting the patriarchal God and his ever-acquisitive priesthoods, after the latter spent centuries demolishing women's own religions. A human analogy is found in the Bible: Yahweh directed his warriors to take heathen girl children as their household slaves and concubines, after raping and killing the girls' mothers (Num. 31:17–18; Judges 21:10–12).

If a few women today talk of resurrecting the long-since raped and killed Divine Mother, many churchmen believe they can be ignored as too few, and usually too poor, to matter. Churches go on enjoying the faithful service of their unpaid ladies' auxiliaries and maintain the conventional idea that women who recognize no church, or who call themselves witches and Goddess worshipers, are only lunatic-fringe cultists, misled by some diabolical power into making fools of themselves.

In one sense, women may again play into patriarchal hands when they leave conventional religion behind and begin to study, work, and play with the older matriarchal concepts. Most Goddess worshipers emphasize such traits as human warmth, love, sensitivity, generosity, and nonjudgmental acceptance. Lo and behold, the same traits were always urged upon Christian women too. Through the course of European history, by the golden rule standard, women were the only true Christians. Their men may have talked fine rhetoric about loving their enemies and giving away all their worldly goods; but in practice, Christian men slaughtered their enemies in unending wars, crusades, and persecutions, while their church was the richest institution in a Europe foully poisoned by the abject poverty of its general population.

Women were poorest of all under Christian laws that allowed them to own nothing, not even their own clothing. Yet women certainly tried to love their enemies, the men who married them in order to use them as draft animals and breeding stock, often beating them into submission and subjecting them to repeated marital rape, with the church's blessings.

So what's different about today's women telling each other to be patient, loving, nurturant, and sensitive to others' needs, in honor of a Great Mother instead of a Great Father? Perhaps the major difference is that women are teaching each other to accept themselves and other women, nonmembers of the in-group, more easily than they used to. Gone are the days when a "respectable" woman would shrink in loathing from a prostitute. Women are learning to recognize their sisterhood under the skin, and to know there are many different ways of being victimized.

However, this attitude change offers no real threat to the male establishment, which need not care if victimized women are feeling sorrier for each other than they once did. The female "power" women talk about is still figurative, not literal. Practical men of the world don't believe the women who call themselves witches can cast real spells, invoke real spirits, or perform real miracles. In their view, it's all self-delusion and folly.

Here lies one of the most vulnerable areas of the women's spirituality movement. Some members advocate a complete return to primitive shamanistic beliefs and practices, on the ground that women should trust "feminine" magic and intuition ahead of "masculine" science and logic. They argue that reasoning, linear thinking, numerical calculation, and other types of mentation leading to our modern technological horrors are "masculine" functions of the left cerebral hemisphere, whereas the right cerebral hemisphere controls "feminine" functions like insight, imagination, emotion, creativity, responsiveness, and the cyclic, unified, holistic world view. Believing that the former mode has been overdeveloped in our society at the expense of the latter, they may rebel against the disciplines of formal education by deliberately embracing the irrational.

An erroneous new stereotype arises here, which may endanger women's ultimate goals. No one would advocate a total return to the Stone Age way of life which was, in the famous phrase, nasty, brutish, and short. We have long since learned that no amount of herbal poultices can cure peritonitis; that invocations alone can't mend a fractured skull; and that tuberculosis is not caused by demons. In any direct contest between science and faith, science will win. For four hundred years the church condemned Galileo's telescopic discoveries, yet no ecclesiastical thunders could make the moons of Jupiter disappear or force Venus to stop showing its phases.

A mistake sometimes found in the women's spirituality movement is to assume that patriarchal religions are "left brain" and therefore linear, logical, and lacking true emotional content. In the first place, this dipolar model of the brain is as simplistic and misleading as Freud's division of the personality into superego, ego, and id. In the second place, the major problem with conventional Christianity is not that it is logical, but that it isn't. Virgin births, transubstantiations, resurrections of the flesh, demonic possessions, Eden creations, and miracles make no sense in a scientific world that knows better and can identify these matters as crude fables left over from ages of ignorance.

It should be remembered that in the ancient matriarchal view, retrievable from myths and legends, the Goddess was regarded as the sole origin of orderly, logical thought. Out of her intellectual gifts to women arose such disciplines as mathematics (originally meaning "mother-wisdom"), calendars (originally "lunar" or "menstrual"), systems of measurement, musical and poetic forms, architectural techniques, and many other formal procedures for dealing with both art and nature. The old Greek word *diakosmos,* by derivation a system of order imposed on primal chaos by the Goddess *(Dia),* demonstrates the belief of prehistoric people that rationality was embodied in every child's first teacher, a mother. Indeed, a myth from India indicates that early men believed women's enviable ability to give birth resulted from their superior skill in figuring and in devising systems of measurement.

Even the Judeo-Christian diabolization of Mother Eve retained the ancient perception of the World Mother as the source of enlightenment for all humanity, though Eve had to disobey the orders of the patriarchal God to obtain the knowledge that God wanted to keep hidden from human beings.

Later patriarchal societies have tended to belittle women's intellect by calling it instinctive, unconscious, ultimately irrational. While recognizing women's perceptual acuity, men dismissed it with the rather contemptuous term *intuition* instead of applying its real name, *intelligence.* No matter how often women showed themselves quite capable of rational thought, even capable of cutting through men's more irrational constructs with the hard edge of common sense, female minds were conceded only more emotion to fill the spaces left by less mind. It was another case of damning with faint praise.

Actually, patriarchal cultures built their practical achievements upon those of many earlier, woman-oriented groups, whereas male philosophers tended to introduce more unreason rather than less. For instance, no society was ever more foolishly superstitious or more naively credulous than Christian Europe during its so-called Age of Faith, when truth was discoverable only in the writings of the *fathers* and experimental science was considered a work of the devil.

At the dawn of history, common sense was mangled by the notion of patriarchal gods as universal parents despite their inability to give birth. Myths show that early civilizations had a hard time with that one. People would not accept such deities until many centuries had been devoted to their priests' propaganda campaigns. Even then, verbal contortions and deliberately illogical paradoxes were required to establish the worship of gods who offended the ordinary person's pragmatic understanding of reality.

Today the new morality is offended by a God who condemned all humanity to eternal torture for the sin of seeking enlightenment, then changed his mind and decided to forgive some of the sinners, provided they ate the flesh and blood of his Son, who was also the Divine Father in human form, sent to earth for the express purpose of being sacrificed to himself, an allegedly loving Father who decreed his Son's painful slaying, then punished those who carried out his order. This bloodthirsty Son-killing or self-killing Father, who was one but also three; who professed to want good, but created evil; who pretended to love his mortal children while preparing for them a hell sadistic beyond belief; who ordained all things in advance, yet held humans entirely responsible for the errors he knew they would make; who talked of love and ruled by fear—this deity was hardly a product of rational minds.

As nineteenth-century science began to show, this deity couldn't be supported by logic. His most faithful adherents admitted that he was wildly improbable, standing as a test of their own credulity. This traditional deity was undercut not by any irrationality, but by the inexorable advance of rational science.

Nonetheless, the women's spirituality movement has much to

learn from close study of this God, created in the image of man, for he tells more about men than men can tell about themselves. This God and other violent gods created by men demonstrate that the power of love cannot control men's lust to destroy their own species. It seems the only emotion that controls men effectively is fear.

Over and over, Christian theology assumes that men's morality depends on their fear of God's imaginary hellfire. Theologians seem to think that without such fear, men are incapable of behaving decently toward their fellow creatures. A good man is defined as a God-fearing man. It is said children must have "the fear of God" put into them, usually by punishment, or they will grow up to be criminals and worse.

Ignored are the findings of modern psychology that fear is the basis of violence rather than its antagonist. Men control other men by fear. The ability to intimidate is their definition of power. Some men even try to control their own families by terrorizing wives and children. Instead of trying to understand how others feel and react, they become bullies by using methods they know would work on themselves.

Such men feel contempt for creatures who cannot offer them any physical harm in retaliation. Hence their contempt for women. They would respect women who could or would bully them as their fathers did when they were small. Their cruelty is triggered by an appearance of vulnerability.

Conversely, such men tend to grovel inwardly before their own vision of an omnipotent God, for the very reason that such a God would be both invulnerable and infinitely threatening. Their vision of hell was the quintessential expression of his infinite threat. The horrors perpetrated on earth by their Crusades and Inquisitions were expressions of their fear. They became cruel as naturally and inevitably as a father-battered child grows up to become a batterer.

The women's spirituality movement is faced with a paradox: how to control the morality of men who can only be controlled by fear, while maintaining that rule by fear is evil?

There is the related sticky question of just what kind of leverage women can expect to have, in a society where men control not only the religion, but also the economy, education, communications, technology, and military force. How can powerless women coerce

powerful men into doing what they ought to do for the good of
their race, rather than what they want to do for their own aggran-
dizement?

There is an answer to this question, and it is up to the women's
movement to find and comprehend it, because it lies in the realm
of images: that curiously unreal yet all-important realm that contains the human capacity to establish a culture. To a larger extent
than we realize, culture is symbolism. Most of the contents of our
minds come to us through words and the images that words project. Most powerful however are the preverbal images lying deep
in the unconscious: the remembered experiences of earliest childhood and infancy, which we all hold in common, but do not understand.

Here originate the divine parent figures that our dependence
insists on creating for us. And, despite the apparent triumph of the
Father God that men have given themselves, it is the Mother Goddess who reigns alone on the deepest level, since every mammal
on earth recognizes a mother as its primary or only parent.

The basic fear of any young mammal is abandonment by the
caretaking mother, on whom it is totally dependent. She is everything necessary to life: warmth, nourishment, protection, tactile
and kinesthetic stimulation, training in the skills of survival. To be
rejected by her is to die.

Human infants can die of insufficient mothering even when their
physical needs are adequately met. Monkeys may survive an infancy of insufficient mothering, but when they grow up, as laboratory studies have shown, they are incapable of mating.

It is becoming clearer that in the human species also, there are
profound connections between adult sexuality and mother-child
bonding in the first year of life. Grown men relate sexually to
women in ways that seem rooted in the mother-child bond: their
breast obsession, for instance. Since women become "mother," or
caretaker, their sexual behavior is more complex. Their sensual,
sexual responses recall the acute whole-body sensitivity of the
female infant. What either sex is least able to bear in sexual relationships is total rejection. Clinging together physically, psychically, and emotionally constitutes that ill-defined, but apparently
essential, condition known as love.

This is a key to the means of control that women might exert toward men, if women evolve a future system of moral standards. For two thousand years, Western men utilized "God's love" as a reward for obeying the rules of their society, and God's rejection (abandonment to hell) as the worst imaginable threat of punishment. Similarly, earlier societies utilized the blessings or curses of the Goddess to even greater effect, since she more clearly represented the ever-desired mother.

On the spiritual level, women can kill with rejection. Women can kill the patriarchal God both literally and figuratively—in the case of a deity, these terms are synonymous—simply by rejecting him. Medieval churchmen knew this perfectly well. That is why their attacks on women who might be even suspected of rejecting their God took on the insane brutality of panic. The things they did to "witches" certainly could be described as overkill.

Women's most feared power over men, then, is the power to say no. To refuse to take care of men. To refuse to service them sexually. To refuse to buy their products. To refuse to worship their God. To refuse to love them. Every rapist knows that sex can be forced, but no power in the world can force love from any woman who wishes to withhold it.

Men may talk complacently of their conviction that God loves them; but in reality, what they need in their daily lives is the love of women. If it is denied, most men feel somehow incomplete as human beings. This is why nearly all the patriarchal rules for feminine behavior aim at immobilizing each woman in the service of a man, so she can have no economic, sexual, or intellectual freedom to say no.

The patriarchal God has always been a primary tool of this effort. It was absolutely necessary to convince women that God wanted them to do what men wanted them to do, since women were hardly inclined by nature to make slaves of themselves or their children.

With the decline of blind faith during the so-called Enlightenment of the nineteenth century, the new male-dominated pseudoscience of psychiatry replaced God with a new gospel of female masochism, passivity, and emotional instability, with the aim of convincing women afresh of their "natural" dependence on men.

The women's spirituality movement denies such male-serving stereotypes, asserting that women are quite capable of controlling their own lives, making their own decisions, and also deciding how men should behave in order to qualify as moral individuals. Since male morality has failed to control its own acquisitiveness and violence, many women now believe that such control must be imposed from another source. The only source immediately at hand is the sex that nurtures the life of the future, thinks with common sense, considers most hierarchical structures inequitable, and generally hates violence.

The real power that women can exert through psychological archetypes may be retrieved from pre-Christian symbol systems, where no attempt was made to conceal it. However, since these systems were devised in prescientific ages, they often confused real power with erroneous theories. One of the dangers of resurrecting the Goddess archetype lies in its proximity to unscientific and unworkable explanations of the natural world, which must be carefully weeded out, so the valid core concepts may shine forth.

During the Age of Reason, European intelligentsia began to reject patriarchal religion on the ground that it doesn't make sense, which led to various agnostic or freethought movements. Modern civilization would have no cogent reason to accept another kind of religion that doesn't make sense either. Too many lies have already been told in the name of religion. If feminist spirituality is to become firmly established, it must be at bottom rational. This means taking account of what the archetypes signify, in terms of the collective human psyche that evolved them, rather than as explanations of the external natural world.

On the psychological level, then, it will be necessary for women to investigate that part of pre-Christian religion that was most particularly obliterated because men found it most intimidating: the negative aspect of the all-powerful Mother, who embodied the fearful potential for rejection, abandonment, death. Most ancient religions made a definite symbolic place for this darker feminine image. It was perceived as present and powerful, in equal proportion to the beautiful, sensual, divine giver of birth, light, love, and nurture—just as night must coexist with day, winter with summer. Ancient cyclic images of the cosmos necessarily recognized a recessive period in every cycle, since a continuously affirmative system (such as the Christian notion of heaven) would cease to be cyclic at all.

Witch persecutions were one more manifestation of men's never-ending effort to deny that negative archetype, the Crone Mother who can destroy. Modern male prejudices against aging women represent another manifestation of the same effort. Such prejudices are rarely studied with any degree of frankness. Freud himself was subject to this male fear, but made heroic efforts to suppress his own knowledge of it.

It has been suggested that such hidden, unacknowledged fears are the very forces that drive men to kill other members of their own species in such appalling numbers, as in war, dividing them into We and They, the latter always viewed as expendable. Part of the vast cultural attempt to deny death is the possibility of inflicting death on others in order to purge it from oneself.

The time is long overdue for the human mind to achieve a valid grasp of these matters. We must comprehend the sources and meanings of our own symbol systems before our race destroys itself through ignorance of its own motivations, through lack of self-knowledge and self-control, and through inability to confront its own fear.

The possibility of a future true morality is contained not in the fear of God, but in the still unknown meanings of the old, grim Goddess who represented fear itself. She is the one we most need to understand: not the pretty Virgin; not the fecund Mother; but the wise, willful, wolfish Crone.

The Crone was the feminine equivalent of the old man with a white beard who lived up in the sky and commanded armies of angels: that is, a naive symbol of a collective idea. The idea was evolved by women, not men. The symbol represented a uniquely feminine world view, unaltered by men, who feared the Crone image enough to leave it alone. They assimilated the Virgin and Mother phases of the ancient Goddess to Christianity, combined them, and deprived the combination of divine status; but the Crone phase was too darkly threatening to be so handled.

Like old women in general, the symbolic Old Woman haunted the fringes of Western culture, largely unnoticed and unacknowledged except when her "witchcraft" aroused a panic. Because she retained so much of her original prepatriarchal character, she is a valuable study object for modern feminists desirous of reassessing the female image.

The Crone is of value, too, as an indication of the power of women's nay-saying, hence of their best hope of exerting control in a male-dominated world where they are expected always to say yes. The Crone's title was related to the word *crown,* and she represented the power of the ancient tribal matriarch who made the moral and legal decisions for her subjects and descendants. As an embodiment of wisdom, she was supposed to have written the first tablets of the law and punished the first sinners. She also established the cyclic system of perpetual becoming, whereby every temporary living form in the universe blends eventually into every other form, nothing is unrelated, and there can be no hierarchy of better or worse, We and They. It was a philosophical system profoundly opposed to the ones devised by men.

Perhaps necessarily, the Crone is being rediscovered by a world that male systems appear to be pushing toward a brink of disaster without parallel in history or prehistory. It has been said before, that archetypes suppressed by any culture will tend to arise again and again, threatening the establishment that suppressed them. At present it is not clear just what hidden psychological forces threaten our world; but we must try to find out.

The Old Woman, who acknowledges no master, may be our best guide in this long, dark, labyrinthine spiritual journey.

2

The Lost Crone

2

The collective unconscious of man holds a secret that woman seldom realizes. The secret may be too irrational for the practical female mind to grasp readily. However, those exquisitely detailed mirrors of the unconscious, mythology and religion, demonstrate the secret so thoroughly that it can hardly be doubted.

The secret is this. In the hidden depths of men's minds, images of women are often identified with images of death.

We know of the *vagina dentata,* that toothy female genital mouth said to swallow a man and reduce him to nothing, just as—even without teeth—it can take away the power of his erection. The *vagina dentata* is perhaps a silly image, not even amenable to simple fakery, as are ghosts and dragons, relics and resurrections. Yet this improbable image is found everywhere in the world, in all times and places where men have tried to understand their world with the help of symbols.

Chinese sages insisted that women's genitals are both "gateways to immortality" and "executioners of men."[1] Natives of New Guinea called female genitals "as dangerous as an open grave." The Maori belief in a literal born-again reincarnation led to description of a vagina as "the house of the dead," that is, a place of ghosts seeking rebirth.[2]

Moslems had so much secret fear of the mouthlike vulva, which they called "insatiable," that by extension they also labeled women's mouths obscene. Moslem women were forced to hide their mouths when they appeared in public.[3] The men also persuaded themselves that a vulva-mouth could bite off a man's eyesight, so a man who looked at female genitals could go blind.[4]

Ancient Greek men personified their own terror of women's "devouring" sexuality as the hungry Lamiae, she-demons whose name meant either vaginas or gullets, also known as *Empusae* or "forcers-in."[5] These were responsible for loss of semen in wet dreams, like the succubae of later Christian legend, who were said to eat men's souls in the same manner. Sex was not always viewed as male "possession" of a female. Sometimes it was the other way round. Early Assyrian and Babylonian writings refer to sexual intercourse as a "taking" by the female, and a "being taken" or "putting forth" by the male.[6] On consideration, this does seem a more logical picture.

Many such images arose from men's apparently universal sense of diminishment in sexual climax, still often called man's little death.[7] It was once a common opinion that sex allows a woman to consume some portion of a man's vital spirit, so she is fed while he is deprived and brought another step closer to real death. This notion led to a thousand forms of asceticism and celibacy, some of which are with us yet, and all of which fostered philosophies fated to poison sexual love.

The notion also led to a widespread belief that a woman who outlived her husband had somehow used up his life force and killed him, even if unintentionally. Hence the mistreatment of widows in patriarchal cultures, including our own, which imposes economic hardship on many a widow, on the ground that she never earned a pension by productive work—even though she may have toiled twice as hard as her spouse to provide the total support system his productivity required.

Many men still have the vague unconscious impression that if a husband dies, his wife's support system has somehow failed him, and she is to blame. On some level of unreason, man still expects woman the life giver to maintain life indefinitely. We have not fully outgrown the typically primitive idea that every death is a result of malice, or that men could live forever if they were not attacked by female powers. There are cultures where every widow is automatically suspected of having murdered her spouse. The European custom of penitential dress in the form of "widow's weeds" has its counterpart among the Haviks, who force widows to remove their ornaments, shave their heads, and wear a costume of degradation. Even so, a widow is regarded as dangerous. It is claimed that she must kill one more victim each year to keep herself alive.[8]

From a similarly primitive viewpoint, our own Judeo-Christian tradition insisted that woman was the universal death bringer. God imposed death on the world only because of the disobedience of Eve; so said early rabbinic commentators and fathers of the church. Tertullian said it was entirely Eve's fault that death came to destroy "God's image, Man," and that "even the Son of God had to die."[9]

The *Book of Enoch,* the wisdom of Jesus ben Sirach, pseudepigrapha, and early apocalyptic writings said woman (Eve) was responsible for the death of every man.[10] In the fifth century A.D. a church council declared it heresy to call death a natural necessity, rather than the result of Eve's sin.[11] Some modern theologians are still trapped by such nonsense, claiming that the mythic unpleasantness in Eden resulted in death as a "demonstration" of human sin. "Death is guilt made visible," says theologian Karl Rahner.[12]

Few dared suggest that an overly harsh God may have been at fault, instituting capital punishment for every living creature, because the first mother of one single species ate a forbidden apple. Timorous men granted gods the right to be unjust or cruel without limit. When analyzed psychologically, this particular aspect of patriarchal imagery yields some surprising results.

Much of Western patriarchal prejudice against women can be traced, through labyrinthine pathways of the unconscious, to symbolic feminization of man's ultimate fear: the fear of his own final nonexistence. To Christian men, even a hell of eternal torture seemed preferable to this. The prejudice became especially virulent in attacks on older women, millions of whom met gruesome, agonizing deaths when men chose to view them as witches.

The secret image of the old woman as Mother Death, the Crone, once found conscious recognition everywhere, because it was essential to older religious systems. Patriarchal faiths undertook to eradicate it, laboring in ignorance of what we are just beginning to rediscover: namely, that archetypes can be suppressed but not destroyed, and their suppression can be socially catastrophic. The image of the death-bringing Crone was such an archetype. Though now lost, this image is in need of rediscovery. Unlike the patriarchal gods who succeeded her, the Crone did not encourage holocausts of war and murder in the futile effort to exorcise each man's fear of death by projecting it on others.

The idea of blaming death on the Mother of All Living was not original with Judeo-Christian antifeminism. In some form, not necessarily antifeminist, it may be found in primitive, pagan, classical, Oriental, and Indo-European religions. The basic idea was incorporated into fundamental worship of the Great Mother, which predated recognition of fatherhood, throughout the world.

To the ancients it seemed obvious that the female principle is the only one that gives life. But every life so given mysteriously bears within it the seed of its own death. Thus, the life given and nurtured by the Great Mother, through the agency of the earthly mother, is necessarily finite. Mother gives a life that will be ended by death. Greedy man wanted more than this "spangle of existence." Growing too soon old and too late (if ever) enlightened, the one animal on earth able to realize its inevitable death often wasted its best years devising mental tricks to deny that realization.

At every stage, man's images of woman were inextricably entangled with these ideas. First came the stage of birth giving and nurturing. Woman formed each new human life from her own interior "wise blood"—that magical, taboo substance once believed to have descended from the moon, ever repeating the lunar phases. A mother voluntarily gave her whole attention to her helpless infant, day and night, for years, until the child could take a gradually increasing part in the life of the community. Ancient Hindu scriptures declared that a mother should be honored one thousand times more than a father because of her irreplaceable benevolence in bearing, nurturing, and training her child.[13]

Hindu sages rightly perceived that all forms of love began with the complex interaction of sensuality, body language, compassion, play, reassurance, tenderness, verbal communication, and other facets of mother-child bonding, which they combined under the term *karuna*, "mother love." They already knew what has been proved again in our own time: that development of adult sexuality and sociability depends largely on mother-child interaction early in life. It has been noted that adult sexual behavior often takes on infantile patterns such as breast sucking, cuddling, pet names, and baby talk. At least in part, a sexual relationship reverts to the period in life when learning to play with Mother was, in effect, learning to live with the world.

After birthing, bringing up, and sexual bonding, man's view of woman edged toward her other matriarchal roles of judge, advisor, wisewoman, caretaker of the sick, comforter of the dying, funerary priestess, intercessor with the gods. She who introduced life also introduced death. Karmic balance ruled the cyclic patterns of female-oriented religions. Every burgeoning was inevitably followed by corresponding decline. There could be no dawn without dusk, no spring without fall, no planting without harvest, no birth without death. The Goddess never wasted her substance without recycling. Every living form served as nourishment for other forms. Every blossom fed on organic rot. Everything had its day in the sun, then gave place to others, which made use of its dying.

This naturalistic world vision was pushed aside by rising patriarchal religions, which were basically antinature, viewing all flesh as sinful and all death as punishment rather than a universal recycling process. To such as the Jain Buddhists, Zoroastrians, Essenes, Manichaeans, and early orthodox Christian sects, earthly life was not an end in itself. It was only a testing ground for the soul, which could theoretically conquer death and attain a permanent, static Nirvana, or paradise, or possibly an eternity of torture. They said the only real purpose of living was to decide one's status in the afterworld. This was supposed to give meaning to an otherwise meaningless existence.

To enforce their view, patriarchal priesthoods had to eliminate the "Thousand-Named Goddess" whose images were embedded in the cultures of the whole Eurasian land mass. The religion of the Great Mother was theologically very different from that of the Heavenly Father—whose remoteness from the earth was implied by his very title. The Great Mother *was* the earth, as well as the sea, the moon, the Milky Way, the elements, mountains, rivers, aniconic, or nonrepresentational, stones, vegetation, women, time, fate, intelligence, birth, love, and death. Her scriptures credited her with the initial creation of the universe and everything in it, as well as the ongoing creation and temporary preservation of each individual creature. She was also the destroying Crone, who brought an end to each life and eventually would destroy the universe itself at doomsday, only to prepare a new creation in her next cycle.

This many-named Goddess was the first Holy Trinity. Her three major aspects have been designated Virgin, Mother, and Crone; or, alternatively, Creator, Preserver, and Destroyer. The same trinitarian pattern can be traced in all the Goddess figures of India, Arabia, Egypt, the Middle East, Aegean and Mediterranean cultures, and among Celtic and Teutonic peoples of northern Europe.

In India, one of the earliest homes of fully developed Goddess worship, within historical times, a Brahman priesthood tried to replace the original female trinity with three male gods, Brahma the Creator, Vishnu the Preserver, and Shiva the Destroyer. However, the Goddess's devotees protested and fought back. They wrote in the Tantrasara that the Triple Goddess alone was the One Primordial Being, the Creatress of the three gods themselves.[14] Brahma, Vishnu, Shiva, and all other gods were born of her "beginningless and eternal" body. At the end of the world they would again disappear into her cosmic being. The Nirvana Tantra said other gods had no more chance of understanding the Mother's fathomless nature than a mud puddle in a cow's hoofprint could understand the fathomless depth of the sea. "The gods themselves are merely constructs out of Her maternal substance."[15]

In some areas, the Goddess was represented as three-faced or three-headed, like the Hebe-Hera-Hecate trinity of archaic Greece. In other areas, she was three individuals who were still somehow one, embodying the same spirit like the grandmother, mother, and daughter of the matrilineal clan. The Goddess Uni, Mother of the Uni-verse, was a pre-Roman form of Italy's Capitoline Triad, formerly composed of Juventas the nubile Virgin, Juno the preserving Mother, and Minerva the all-wise Crone.

Virgin and Mother aspects of the ancient Goddess were merged and adopted by Christianity about the fifth century A.D., after much opposition from earlier church fathers, who insisted that Virgin Mother Mary must never be worshiped, and must never receive the older Goddess's title, Mother of God.[16] Despite such opposition, the people demanded a Christianized version of their ancient Goddess. At Ephesus, sacred city of the Divine Mother worshiped by "all Asia and the world" (Acts 19:27), a council of bishops in 432 A.D. was besieged by crowds calling for restoration of their Goddess. Fearing mob violence if the demand was not met, the council responded by instituting the cult of Mary in the Goddess's Ephesian temple.

As one of the earliest known centers of Marian worship, Ephesus presents an interesting example of deliberate amputation of the Crone aspect, formerly thought essential to comprehension of the trinitarian Goddess. According to Greek tradition, the holy city of Ephesus was founded more than a thousand years before the

Christian era. Its reigning deity was the Amazons' supreme Goddess, called Artemis in Greece and Troy, Diana in Rome, Astarte in Byblos, Aphrodite in Syria, Isis in Egypt, and so on: She had a different name in every language or local dialect.

Like other forms of the Great Mother, the Ephesian Goddess had her Virgin, Mother, and Crone facets, often signified by the new moon, full moon, and waning moon. Her Virgin form entered classic Greco-Roman myth as the familiar huntress of the silver bow (lunar crescent). She was often presented as sexually pure, though older legends made her the sun god's sister-spouse and an ardent patron of sexuality, marriage, and childbirth. Such apparent incongruity is explained by the fact that the Goddess's Virgin form was always the birth giver (or Creatress) in pagan myths as well as in their Christian derivative. Her offspring was some form of the sacrificial god whose blood "redeemed" his followers. He was Adonis the Lord, or Actaeon the stag king, or Aleyin the Lamb of God, or Christos the Anointed One. His deaths and resurrections were enacted at regular intervals, at Ephesus and everywhere else around the eastern Mediterranean, for thousands of years before Christianity swallowed them all.

The Mother aspect of the Great Goddess nurtured not only the sacred king or the sacrificial animal representing him, but all men and all animals. She was the Preserver whose ever-flowing breasts symbolically provided food for every life form. At Ephesus, as elsewhere, she was called Mother of the Animals. Her most famous Ephesian image had a torso entirely covered with breasts, showing her ability to nurture the whole world. Later students of classical mythology found it hard to reconcile this vision of superfecund motherhood with their own vision of the pure, girlish, untouchable Virgin Huntress.[17]

In fact the Huntress character belonged originally to the Goddess's third *persona,* the dangerous Crone, who often merged with the Virgin because of the cyclic nature of her trinity, a closed loop of alternating forms like the phases of the moon. Mother Death was often represented as a huntress, an implacable Fate hunting down men and beasts. Egyptians sometimes called her Sati the Huntress. In Rome she was the Venus whose worship used to be called venery, which meant (and still means) hunting, as well as the sexual rites traditionally attributed to her.

Confusion of the Virgin and the Crone led to a long-standing error in the myth of Mycenaean Demeter, one of the oldest Earth Mother figures, known in Crete as Rhea and in Latium as Ceres. Demeter was a trinity collectively named Mother De, that is, the delta or triangle, a basic female symbol throughout the ancient world. The delta was a hieroglyphic sign for "woman," representing her genital Holy Door (as shown by the triangular entrance-ways of Mycenaean tombs); sages of Southeast Asia called it the Triangle of Life, or Primordial Image.[18] Originally, each point of Demeter's triangle was personified. There was Kore the Virgin, Pluto the Mother, and Persephone the Crone, whose name means "Destroyer." Yet the maiden Kore was said to be the same as Persephone in classic myth. Both names were given to Demeter's daughter, while the maternal Pluto—whose name formerly referred to the "abundance" of her overflowing breasts—was de-sexed and recast in the role of an underworld king, the spouse of Persephone as Queen of the Shades.

At Ephesus, the Virgin-Huntress-Crone was often called the Widow, since she stood for the ritual death of her son-spouse, the sacred king. The Greek Mother of Gods also held the title of Widow, especially in her temple at Stymphalus.[19] In sacred dramas, the Widow chose her new sacred king at the foot of the pillar or cross where her former king was sacrificed. Sometimes he too took a trinitarian form, so there were three victims at once.[20] The scene might have borne a more than passing resemblance to the three crosses of Christian iconography.

A curious circumstance that Christian scholars chose to ignore was the further resemblance between the three Marys at the foot of Jesus' cross, and the traditional pagan tableau of the three Moerae (Fates) attending the sacred king's immolation. Northern Europe showed the same Triple Goddess as three Norns (Fates) at the foot of the World Tree where the Heavenly Father hung dying, sometimes in the form of his own son.[21]

All three aspects of the Mother were required at the sacred drama, where gods died to beget themselves for another rebirth. We find early Christian writings that identify all three Marys at the crucifixion with one another, as if they were one more version of the ancient female trinity.[22] There was a Virgin Mother, a Dearly Beloved (Magdalene), and a third, more shadowy Mary. The Coptic *Gospel of Mary* said they were all one.[23] Even as late as the Renaissance, a trinitarian Mary appeared in the *Speculum beatae Mariae* as Queen of Heaven (Virgin), Queen of Earth (Mother), and Queen of Hell (Crone).[24]

This strange triple Mary may have been worshiped at Ephesus in Crone form, like the famous Widow, according to the widely prevalent legend that Jesus's mother lived at Ephesus in her old age.[25] She would have taken on something of the character of the Grandmother, another title for Diana of Ephesus. Significantly, the Christian version of the "Grandmother of God" received the same name as the Ephesian Goddess: Di-anna, or Dinah, or Anna, assimilated into Christian lore as the Virgin's mother.[26] Some sources gave her name as Dinah, others Hannah, Anna, or Anne. All were derived from the pagan "heavenly mother" Ana, an elder version of the Semitic-Amorite Virgin Mari.[27]

Mari or Mara meant not only the Virgin, but also the Death Goddess or Huntress. Like the variant Mary, it was a word for the briny sea, which ceremonially swallowed up a number of dying savior figures including Osiris and Adonis, said to have been born in Bethlehem of the blue-robed Marine Aphrodite. Saint Jerome said the birth of this pagan god took place in precisely the same cave where the infant Christ also came into the world.[28] The name of the sea-mother Mara was also taken by the biblical Naomi when she entered her Crone state of widowhood (Ruth 1:20). In the legend of Buddha it was the name of a death spirit. Combined with another Amorite or Canaanite name of the Goddess, Anatha, this mysterious Mara represented the formal death curse given in the Gospels as Maranatha (1 Cor. 16:22).

This may have referred indirectly to a common element of the sacred drama. The Crone, or her representative, laid a solemn curse on the dying god just before his sacrifice.[29] In a similar Jewish custom, a curse was laid on the head of the scapegoat which was to die in atonement for the sins of the community. The Canaanite Goddess Anatha laid the curse on her dying god Aleyin, whose reed scepter was broken, and who was forsaken by his heavenly father, in the Canaanite forerunner of the Christian crucifixion story. Offering himself as "the lamb to be sacrificed in expiation," Aleyin dissolved into his alter ego Mot, the Death King, only to be resurrected again with the vegetation of a new season.[30]

Gods who played the part of sacrificial offerings would have been described by the same word in both Greece and Rome, *anathemata*, "those who are accursed," in the sense of something specially chosen and tabooed for a supernatural purpose.[31] The same dual meaning could be found in Latin *sacer*, both "sacred" and "accursed"; in other words, untouchable, no longer of this world.

The purpose of the Crone's curse was to doom the sacrificial victim inevitably, so no guilt would accrue to those who actually shed his lifeblood. He was already "dead" once the Mother pronounced his fate, so killing him was not real killing. Throughout the ancient world, people believed in the absolute efficacy of a mother's curse. The Markandaya Purana said there was nothing anywhere "that can dispel the curse of those who have been cursed by a mother."[32]

This idea can be traced back to the time before recognition of fatherhood. When mothers were thought the sole makers of life, they were credited with the power to destroy what they made. Ceremonial propitiation of dead forebears (that is, "fore-bearers") probably arose as an attempt to ward off mothers' death curses from beyond the grave. If the curse of death was not imposed by a real mother—alive or dead—then it was attributed to her collective image, the World Mother in her Destroyer aspect.

Here we have one of the Crone's most important metaphorical functions. Unlike later patriarchal societies, which considered a Goddess only as the passive, humble, ever-benevolent Mother beloved, like Mary, prepatriarchal societies frankly envisioned her actively sexual and destructive sides. In nature, they reasoned, destruction is as necessary to cosmic balance as creation. Thus, the Goddess tirelessly created and destroyed, destroyed and created. "She eliminated the old and useless, those who had performed their role in life, while at the same time presiding over the perpetual renewal of life by means of love and regeneration."[33] She gave the blessing of life, followed by the curse of death.

Moreover, her ultimate curse would devour the very gods themselves, when the Goddess decided to initiate doomsday. She would curse all men at once, when they were led astray by warlike gods, becoming universally violent and greedy, neglecting the feminine principles of *karuna* (mother-inspired love), clan loyalty, and devotion to their mothers and wives.[34]

Similar doomsday myths featuring the Crone's curse are found in areas as widely separated as India and Scandinavia. Such myths seem to have had a common origin in prehistoric times. According to the Scandinavian version, spirits called up by the curse, to bring on the final cataclysms and the death of the gods, came from "hot lands in the south" named Mutspellheim, "the Land of Mother's Curse." In that same southern land, images of the Destroying Mother are still potent even today. Her scriptures say that at the end of the world, when the Queen of Gods "chews all things existing with Her fierce teeth," she will be clothed in a garment of blood, presenting a terrifying appearance.[35]

There is more involved here than any primitive eschatology. Psychologists are just beginning to discover that myth is the natural language of the collective unconscious, and that its images hold profound revelations of humanity's mental and emotional development. For example, body and world stand for each other so consistently in the mythological mode that every tale of doomsday can be seen to allegorize the terrifying dissolution of the self in death, while every creation demonstrably presents a buried memory of birth. Both are inextricably entwined with the image of the Mother.

Creation myths the world over begin with chaos, the condition of nondifferentiation between self and other, with "primordial elements" suggesting the uterine environment: darkness, churning, the "eternal flux," the maternal ocean of blood holding all future forms in formless potential. Often there was a reference to a lesser entity inside another, greater one, "when darkness was enveloped in Darkness," and the future cosmos was still united with the Formless Mother.[36]

The Bible calls this Formless Mother *tehom*, "the Deep," a Hebrew derivation of her earlier Sumero-Babylonian name, Tiamat, which might be rendered also Dia Mater, "Goddess Mother." Even though "without form and void," as in Genesis, she knew how to create the *Diakosmos*, the Pythagoreans' "Order of the Goddess."[37] At the end of time, according to Oriental sages, she would destroy the same cosmos and again resume her "dark formlessness."[38]

Several creation myths said the Goddess brought order out of her own chaos by her rhythmic movements on or within the primal Deep.[39] Indeed, how else would a human mind symbolize the forgotten-but-unforgotten first experience of birth: rhythmic expulsive movements of the womb? The creative process was crowned with the sudden appearance of "light," like the forgotten-but-unforgettable first impact of light on eyes that saw only darkness before.

Our patriarchal Bible predictably attributes to the male God the invocation *Fiat lux* (Let there be light). However, earlier images of the Goddess bore titles showing that she was the original light bringer, like Mater Matuta, "Mother of the First Dawn." Egyptians said the light of the sun rose on earth for the first time from the womb of the Goddess.[40] Under her Roman title of Juno Lucina, "Bringer of Light," she not only mothered the light of the world but also "opened the eyes" of newborn children with her gift of sight.[41]

In similar vein, myths of doomsday may be recognized as expressions of the fear of death. Their unquenchable fires, all-consuming floods, crumbling mountains, breaking continents, stars falling from the sky, and so on simultaneously conceal and reveal the certain knowledge human beings have but do not want: knowledge of their own ultimate destruction. That sad knowledge is acutely perceived by humans alone among all the animals on earth, and may be called the true curse under which we live—part of the price we pay for intelligence. We are forced to recognize the impermanence of our existence, regardless of our personal wishes.

The mythic-psychological doomsday comes for each person, though not necessarily for all together. Man has usually sought a crumb of comfort in the notion of a universal apocalypse; apparently one's own dissolution seems more tolerable if one can end the world with it. Men especially dislike the thought that after each one ceases to exist, others will continue in the usual way, soon filling the empty space. Along this line of thought a man is pushed toward the conclusion that no matter how precious his life is to him, no matter how he strives, accomplishes, and hoards to validate that life and protect it against every assault, still in the cosmic scale it weighs no heavier than the life of a hyena or a scorpion. Man's ego seizes almost any idea, however improbable, to evade this sort of conclusion.

The older, matriarchal view of the Crone accompanied a philosophy less centered in the ego, more accepting of natural cycles. Just as seed developed into ripening fruit, then withered away, so growing up would pass through maturity into growing old. No power in earth or heaven could rescind this cyclic law, which is why the Goddess of waxing and waning was thought more powerful than any god. As the birth-giving Virgin and the death-dealing Crone were part of one another, death and life together were like the new seed within the withered fruit, so visions of the young Goddess invariably merged with the old one.

The Crone was the most powerful of the Goddess's three personae. Seen in myth after myth as an old woman, she was yet stronger than any god. Under one of her Teutonic names, Elli or "Old Age," in a wrestling match she conquered even the god of strength, Thor himself.[42]

In a similar Celtic version, Morgan Le Fay, or Morgan the Fate, became humanized by monkish scribes as a witch sister of King Arthur. Nevertheless, they wrote: "Morgan the Goddess is her name, and there is never a man so high and proud but she can humble and tame him."[43] She was also the Fata Morgana, whose appearance meant death. She was greatly feared in Italy, France, and Ireland.

As Atropos the Cutter, the old-woman third of the Greek trinity of Fates or Moerae, the Crone snipped the thread of every life with her inexorable scissors. As Nemesis, the "inescapable" Fate among the gods, she overruled the will even of Heavenly Father Zeus.[44] Taken as aids to comprehension of reality, such symbols were accurate enough. Old age indeed weakens even the strongest, and death indeed conquers even the greatest.

Until the Crone figure was suppressed, patriarchal religions could not achieve full control of men's minds. Such religions tended not only to ascetic rejection of the physical experiences of life, but also to fearful rejection of the Divine Old Woman, and by extension of old women generally.

The horrors of Europe's five-century witch mania were rooted in this ideological effort. Men's inner fears, cannily inflated by a woman-despising church, led to unprecedentedly relentless persecution of the aging mothers of an entire civilization. Women still don't really know why it happened. Male historians have refrained from telling them much about it; and scholars have yet to develop the kind of insight needed to analyze it.

Figures of myth may be the best or even the only route to such insight. At present, such figures dwell in a strange twilight zone between the literal existence accorded them by childlike believers and the purely figurative existence accorded them by poetic allegorists. Apart from Jung and his followers, few have yet perceived the psychological dimension where such figures may be said to dwell in a real, but wholly interior, landscape (or heavenscape). Characters of gods and goddesses are obvious human projections onto a nonhuman universe. The ways in which any given culture chooses to relate to them affects and reflects the ways in which the people of that culture relate to each other.

Our culture's official rejection of the Crone figure was related to rejection of women, particularly elder women. The gray-haired high priestesses, once respected tribal matriarchs of pre-Christian Europe, were transformed by the newly dominant patriarchy into minions of the devil. Through the Middle Ages this trend gathered momentum, finally developing a frenzy that legally murdered millions of elder women from the twelfth to nineteenth centuries.

The sixteenth-century physician Johann Weyer was severely reprimanded for venturing to suggest that executed witches were really harmless old women who confessed to impossible crimes only because they were driven mad by unendurable tortures.[45] As a rule, the real offenses of such women were (1) living, or trying to live, independent of male control; and (2) being poor.

Historical writings show that many women entered the state of widowhood with frank relief, even joy, after a lifetime of male abuse. They resisted remarriage with all their might.[46] They couldn't be coerced into remarriage even by the economic hardship that patriarchal societies usually impose on widows, after they have spent their lives caring for husband and family, living as slaves in the sense that their labor was unpaid, and frequently forced. Such former slaves were further punished in widowhood for not having earned a living. In 1711 Joseph Addison reported that when an old woman became dependent on the charity of the parish, she was "generally turned into a witch" and legally terminated.[47]

The law doesn't murder witches any longer, but modern society does eliminate elder women in a sense. They are made invisible. They rarely appear on those mythic mirrors of our culture, movie and television screens. Men in middle or late-middle age may be seen on screens, in fair numbers, but seldom paired with women their own age. Their romantic partners are often young actresses in their twenties or thirties.

In real life also, signs of old womanhood are not supposed to be seen. Women are socially and professionally handicapped by wrinkles and gray hair in a way that men are not. A multibillion-dollar "beauty" industry exploits women's well-founded fear of looking old. This industry spends megafortunes to advertise elaborately packaged, but mostly useless, products, by convincing women that their natural skins are unfit to be seen in public. Every female face must be resurfaced by a staggering variety of colored putties, powders, and pastes. Instead of aging normally through their full life cycle, women are constrained to create an illusion that their growth process stops in the first decade or two of adulthood.

There is an enormous gulf between a society like this and earlier prepatriarchal societies where elder women were founts of wisdom, law, healing skills, and moral leadership. Their wrinkles would have been badges of honor, not of shame.

Elder women in pre-Christian Europe took charge of religious rites and official sacrifices, from which they read omens on behalf of the community.[48] In the Middle East and Egypt, many elder women were attached to temples of the Goddess, providing a wide range of ecclesiastical services. They were doctors; midwives; surgeons; and advisors on health care, child rearing, and sexuality. They took care of the soul also. They conducted ceremonies for every event from birth to death. As scribes, they kept books for temple and court, wrote histories, maintained vital records and official tables of weights and measures, set up calendars for seasonal religious observances, transcribed and edited scriptures, and administered libraries. Elder women were the religious and secular teachers, universal educators of the young.[49]

In such societies, women were probably even busier in middle age and beyond than in their young-mother years, though their duties and preoccupations changed. Myths often say most of the important inventions of early civilization were made by women in their "years of wisdom." Prepatriarchal China, for instance, believed that all inventions in the fields of medicine, alchemy, nutrition, and food preparation were made by ancient mothers inspired by their Hearth Goddess, described as "a beautiful old woman in red garments."[50]

By contrast, our society regards elder women as decidedly un-beautiful, as well as useless. A traditional housewife under pa-triarchy is left with almost nothing to engage her energy, interest, or ambition at the end of her childrearing years. What she has been taught to think of as her only true fulfillment, the wife-and-mother role, no longer provides satisfaction because it is no longer truly functional.

Her children grow up and leave. Her husband is preoccupied with his career, which usually reaches a peak about this time. During the period when most men receive maximum reward for their lifework, most women lose even the emotional reward of feeling needed. It can become abundantly clear to even the dullest woman that the social importance of her traditional feminine role drops to nearly zero. Thus, it is hardly surprising to find—as recent studies have found—that women are afflicted by midlife depression in direct proportion to their acceptance of the tradi-tional feminine role.[51]

Patriarchal man wishes woman to continue playing the part of the unpaid, but tirelessly devoted, nurturer, long after its biologi-cal foundation has crumbled, and after he ceases to grant her even the specious significance of a sex object. One reason is that patriar-chal man must deny woman the essential later-life functions she naturally assumed in prepatriarchal societies: healer, judge, wise-woman, arbiter of ethical and moral law, owner of the sacred lore, mediator between the realms of flesh and spirit, and—most of all —the functions of the Crone: funerary priestess and Death Mother, controlling the circumstances of death as she controlled those of birth. In their anxiety to deny the Crone archetype through religious imagery, patriarchal societies even denied the fact of death itself.

Hence the typical masculine notion of life as linear, not cyclic, ending not in reabsorption but in eternal stasis, in either heaven or hell. The patriarchs' choice between "good" and "evil" is irrele-vant to the symbolic archetype. The real choice is between the (phallic) line and the (yonic) circle; between death as a mere passage in time to a mysterious imagined world that can never change, and death as a real dissolution according to the law of nature, where change is the only constant.

For good reason the religions of the Goddess viewed existence as *becoming,* not *being.* They saw life as perpetual transition, always changing its colors, shapes, and qualities from moment to moment, like a sunrise or sunset passing from darkness to light, and from light to darkness. That which seemed lifeless would sooner or later become part of something alive. That which lived was, by degrees, becoming dead.

According to the same principle of eternal becoming, the Virgin became the Mother became the Crone. Reincarnation was represented by refertilization of the Virgin. The vital link was the Crone, as Queen of the Shades, Goddess of the Underworld, Lady of Night. It was she who took the soul through dark spaces of nonbeing.

Psychologists have suggested that even patriarchal males unconsciously perceive the world as somehow manipulated by the Mother figure.[52] But man couldn't establish his ideological denial of death unless the Goddess's death-dealing aspect was vehemently denied also. Her traditional appearances, as an old woman, a female corpse, or a mummy, were destroyed as quickly as possible.

She represented the kind of death that our culture wished to conceal, making it invisible as old women are made invisible: the common garden-variety kind of death; death in old age, death from wasting disease, death after slow degeneration of body and mind. Our civilization tries not to acknowledge such death. The kind we are invited to contemplate instead, as "entertainment," is the sudden, violent, bloody kind, in keeping with patriarchal ideals of conflict and aggression. As spectacle, violent death is safe. No matter how dangerous our environment, we seldom believe it will "happen to us." Even men on a battlefield believe they as individuals will survive. It takes time, and the sensations of a weakening body, to become convinced of death's inexorable approach.

So our civilization concealed death in the same way it concealed the aging of women: by complex cosmetic procedures designed to give a false appearance of youth and health, even to a corpse. Medieval doctrines of the resurrection of the flesh led to a modern technology of mummification (embalming) as strangely obsessive as that of the ancient Egyptians. Western Europeans shared with the Egyptians the notion that it was necessary to preserve human remains in as lifelike a condition as possible. Consequently, even today we have such peculiar customs as viewings, to display the mortician's art, when elaborately preserved cadavers publicly present a phony illusion of well-being. The corpse is always pronounced wonderfully peaceful, or looking as if it only sleeps. Once again death is denied, even in its very presence. Survivors are supposed to take comfort from this.

On the other hand, those engaged in the actual process of dying seldom meet with such tender attention as their bodies receive after death. While still alive, able to describe their feelings, to protest their fear, anger, and pain, they find that few of the healthy want to hear them. Care of their deteriorating bodies may be turned over to impersonal professionals who work for pay, not for love. The dying person's desperate emotional needs may go unanswered because others cannot face his weakness.

Patriarchal religions, too, assumed they could provide "comfort" by denying the physical realities of dying. Clergymen delicately administered brief ritual gestures and words that their organizations declared essential for preservation of the soul. They insisted that their routine professional attentions were all-important. But they never held a dying person in their arms, never listened to an expression of feelings, never helped clean up blood, vomit, pus, or feces. As usual, such services were left to women, who—as usual—received scant thanks for providing such real and personal comforts.

It was different when the Crone was recognized as an embodiment of women's care for the dying and the dead. Women not only faced their own aging with pride rather than with shame; they also received due credit as priestesses of the final rites of passage, for their tenderness toward the terminally ill, and for the sacred duties that included their hands-on care.

Just as modern assembly-line medicine often deprived mothers and infants of the true humanness of the birth experience, so it also deprived the dying of attention, because doctors couldn't face their implied reproach. Like many primitives, men of our culture often seemed to have to pretend that death always took them by surprise. Men could allow themselves to inflict death, even on a grand scale, as in war; but they preferred not to see it close up. They could seldom deal with it effectively on an individual basis.

In a number of ways all too familiar to women, modern men often seem unable to deal with biological realities, preferring to live with their own symbol systems which place such biological realities at several removes. Today's men typically give attention and credence to many prescribed, formal fantasies no less unnatural than the fantasy worlds of the earliest patriarchies, when war was first declared on the Goddess image with her triadic birth-giving, nurturing, and death-dealing personae. The one-dimensional images of woman in modern male-dominated media, such as television, offer prime examples.

Recently, a male writer conducted an informal survey to learn how femininity was defined by nearly a thousand people in various walks of life. Men of middle age and older, those most embedded in the patriarchal myth, defined femininity only in relation to a male partner. Women were seen as most "womanly" when being admired and desired by men, while responding to men's sexual approaches, and "during sex." Interviewees seemed to take it for granted that this meant only heterosexual sex. Presumably, a pair of lesbians would not be considered "feminine" when making love to each other, although a woman could be viewed as essentially feminine when a victim of rape. The implication was that feminine meant a passive condition of a sex object, for sexually aggressive women were not so defined no matter how attractive or "sexy" they might be. Younger men more frequently tended to view womanliness simply as a function of humanness, though many in this group also defined the feminine only as a reflection of, or response to, masculine desires.[53] By contrast, it is still common for "masculinity" to be defined only in masculine terms, in relation to its own sex rather than to the opposite sex. Thus, one hears such expressions of masculinity as "a man among men."

In such a society, woman seems to fade into a dark limbo of nonexistence when the spotlight of male attention stops shining on her. Like the philosophical absurdity (male devised) of the universe that couldn't exist unless it was perceived, women in patriarchal society may seem to disappear when entering those times and places of their lives where men play no part—again, in contrast to men, who become most visible in those areas of their lives where women play no part. Naturally, the time of the Crone or widow would be preeminent among periods of female invisibility, for the traditional Crone neither nurtured nor supported males. Indeed, she was quite indifferent to their small secular concerns.

Perhaps the most significant facet of the writer's survey was what male interviewees did *not* say. None of them suggested that a woman might be most "feminine" when focused on the true biological purpose of femininity: bearing, nurturing, and socializing the next generation of her species. This, despite the fact that every female mammal is female for this basic purpose, and virtually indistinguishable from the male in her other life activities; men seem prone to forget that human beings are mammals too.

Apparently, many men regard such acts as birth giving and nursing as somewhat scary or repugnant, and prefer to view as "feminine" only those lesser female functions that relate directly to themselves. For instance, our own society cherishes the curious mass delusion that women's breasts exist primarily for the delectation of adult males, rather than as organs of nurture for infants. Men sometimes are even known to lose interest in the lactating breast, while a nonfunctional breast continues to elicit intense fetishistic response.

It has been suggested that men would rather not contemplate woman-as-mother at all, insofar as biological motherhood distracts woman's attention from them. They respond with jealousy upon discovering that woman, like any other female animal, gives first priority to her young. Adult male sexual behavior has been called a kind of arrested development, the mother-child bond being manipulated for the benefit of grown men, who never cease to demand "maternal solace, nonjudgmental nurturing, and compassion" even from women they have abused.[54] Women who withhold these gifts from men, for any reason including the nurture of their children, may be seen as dangerous aggressors or castrators. The traditional male attitude is ego centered rather than species centered.

The same mix of fear, avoidance, or even contempt that a patriarchal society applies to pregnant, parturient, or lactating women may be applied to old women, who are also locked into the symbolism of motherhood since every man's mother is an older woman. Taken off guard, the aging woman may be astonished and psychically injured by the unexpected hostility she encounters as she slips from full maturity into old age. "Women, when they gear their lives to men and neglect their own inner resources, are caught short by the aging process and must suddenly develop in ways that could not have been foreseen."[55] Patriarchal culture does not provide women with the necessary tools to prepare their Crone persona in advance, to make the transition without trauma. Neither does this culture provide the aging woman with any sense of purpose or usefulness after she is no longer needed by dependent children.

In the normal course of events, a mother precedes her child into the realm of death. Wherever the conventional wisdom claimed that her spirit would live on in that realm, it was naturally assumed that she would continue to guard and assist her children in the land of the dead, just as in the land of the living. The elder mother then took on certain characteristics of a death symbol. Matriarchal traditions of the Celtic "fairy faith" called the country of the dead "Land of Everliving Women." In Brittany, these women were "Our Good Mothers the Fairies."[56] These images rose out of customs of maternal ancestor worship, wherein the ancient mothers of the tribe were placed in the afterworld to receive their descendants into their bosoms, just as later Judeo-Christian visionaries imagined the dead in the bosom of Abraham. Honoring ancestors of only one sex, patriarchal authorities simply left motherhood out of the picture, and settled only "fathers" in heaven to receive the souls of the dead.

This was one more aspect of the strong tendency in patriarchal cultures to ignore or deny biological facts; for, obviously, ancestors could not be solely male. Fear and denial of motherhood was a cultural phenomenon related to men's fear and denial of death. Through such archetypal, esoteric, but very powerful connections, the Crone figure (Mother Death) was gradually diabolized, and eventually denied more firmly than any other tenet of pre-Christian religion. Then, her embodiments on earth inevitably faced some degree of persecution.

Such archetypal connections must be considered in any serious effort to trace to its roots the combination of sexism and ageism that makes elder women the invisible citizens of the modern world. In recent years, feminists have been saying that our society needs less masculine metaphor and more feminine realism in dealing with interpersonal behavior patterns as well as such basic matters as birth, sex, and death. Since men seem unable to handle the idea of death philosophically, some purpose may be served by studying manifestations of the Crone in earlier societies.

Moreover, our civilization needs more of the gut wisdom women achieve simply by living as women: the birth givers; comforters; observers of human nature; and frequently the sole fountainhead of warmth, color, pleasure, and stimulation that gives meaning to the lives of men. Old men are supposed to have acquired enough wisdom to run corporations and governments. It may be that, contrary to popular prejudices, old women acquire even more: perhaps enough wisdom to establish better moral standards for the world.

A first step is to realize that the Crone was once a vital part of divinity, as real to her followers as the Holy Ghost to traditional Christians. In fact, even early Christianity—the nontraditional or Gnostic kind—had its own Crone figure, the feminine forerunner of the later, masculinized Holy Ghost. She was sometimes Sophia, personification of Wisdom; sometimes the Pneuma or Holy Spirit; sometimes Grandmother of God; sometimes the feminine Thought without whom God could not have functioned as a creator. The Gnostic scripture *Trimorphic Protennoia* spoke of her as the typical pre-Christian female trinity: "the one born first of all beings, the one who has three names and yet exists alone, as one. She dwells at all levels of the universe; she is the revealer who awakens those that sleep, who utters a call to remember, who saves."[57]

Certainly, the modern world is in need of saving—not in the esoteric after-death sense, but in the here and now. Certainly, we need to be awakened, and to remember what the Crone used to represent before she fell victim to patriarchal prejudices. In a sense, she was real: as real as any figure of divinity constructed from the collective vision. Her human embodiments were daily seen on earth. Her spirit was known to act, sooner or later, on every living thing without exception. When she was suppressed into invisibility, something important was lost. The ways of thinking and feeling that shaped the Crone were ways that we might do well to understand again.

Of course, we recognize the impossibility of returning, in any literal sense, to an earlier, simpler, or more superstitious mode of life, largely devoid of scientific knowledge. No one would want to slam shut the sophisticated technological windows through which we can now look both outward and inward upon the natural world, from distant galaxies to cell nuclei. We are just beginning to understand our universe a little, and would hardly wish to abandon the effort, to return to the darkness of simplistic anthropomorphized pseudoexplanations for external phenomena.

What is needed is not a withdrawal from analytical thinking, but an extension of such thinking into realms that it has barely touched as yet: the realms of the psychological and social forces that religious archetypes have always mutely represented.

These ideas and images, common to all humanity, have meanings of which we can remain ignorant only at our peril. Like dreams, they never mean exactly what they seem but, properly understood, they bring necessary insights.

In like manner, women have intuitively known what is needed in interpersonal behavior patterns and moral codes, to encourage the optimum quality of life for their children and their society; but this kind of knowing needs formal expression before it can become universally meaningful. Male-dominated culture denied it the formal expression that might have developed into an ethic. The morality supported by past female-oriented religions showed less alienation, more compassion, and a higher degree of practical common sense in dealing with human motivations and responses. Out of just such intuitive understandings of causes and effects in human relationships, women today still automatically enhance the experience of life for their families, without paying strict attention to how they do it. Goddess worship used to be a conscious part of the process. Crone wisdom lay at its source. Fundamentally, the best moral codes have been evolved by ancient peoples who let themselves be guided by their clan matriarchs.

Therefore it seems important to study various manifestations of the Crone figure, and to ponder her archetypal implications; for an archetype, by definition, remains part of the human mind even in a culture that suppresses it. Perhaps a study of the Crone would help bring our own old women out of their closet of suppression, social invisibility, and pejorative labeling. At the same time, it may reveal to men some of their own deepest secrets. In such times as these, we need not to be the slaves of illusion, but to understand what our images mean in human terms, so we may use them as a route to the kind of self-knowledge essential to the building of a better world for the future.

3

The Wise Crone

3

In the beginning there was Mother: sole origin of the ironclad bonds of family and clan that united human groups, making possible such cooperative efforts and activities as would lead to civilization.

Humans are distinguished from other animals by their capacity for verbal communication, learned via the mother-child bond. Verbal communication enables humans to recognize and remember two basic facts of life that are probably absent from the minds of other animals in their maturity: (1) that they have been born of a mother; and (2) that they will die. From collective recognition of these two facts at an early stage in human history arose the spiritual ideas of later societies: all mythologies, all religions, all evasions and denials of death, all transcendent fears and hopes in a species that came to believe it could create by the power of its own word.

Primitive humans saw themselves emerging from a maternal body which, they thought, shaped their very substance out of its own blood by a mysterious intrauterine clotting process. This was the primary meaning of the blood bond, foundation of kinship. Men had no intimate role in blood kinship, except insofar as they too were shaped by it, through the magic of their own mothers. Even when the lesser male role in reproduction was finally recognized, at a late stage of social evolution, it still created no "blood" relation except by a purely verbal convention.

Postpartum development depended on another maternal fluid, milk, which also "clotted" or "curdled" into the substance of the growing body. Men were unable to produce this fluid either. Their envy of such maternal magic was intense, as shown by many mythological sources, including the Bible, which speaks in vain wishfulness of the nursing father carrying a sucking child in his bosom (Num. 11:12), and addresses God as a source of "milk" that creates one's substance (Job 10:10).

Most mysterious of all was the maternal love that prompted women to give of themselves without stint, nursing and caring for helpless babies night and day for many years. Men seem to have watched this process with uncomprehending wonder. Never once, the Egyptian sage Kneusu-Hetep marveled, did a mother's heart neglect the tedious necessities of child care, or impel her to ask herself, "Why should I do this?" By reason of this essential life-giving devotion, a mother was entitled to greater honor than any other creature on earth. In fact, according to Egyptian belief, it was the very quality that united the human mother with the Divine Mother who gave birth to the universe and all its gods at the beginning of time.

Every mammal is born comparatively helpless, dependent on maternal attention: the human mammal most of all. Yet it was no intellectual or cultural recognition of this fact that motivated Stone Age mothers. It was something much deeper, much more awesome to the men who observed but couldn't understand it.

Mother-love was the first of all loves. Physical contacts between mother and child were the foundation of all later interpersonal behavior patterns, including those of sexual behavior. It has been shown that, even among animals, adequate sexual functioning in adulthood depends upon adequate mothering in infancy. The development of the brain and nervous system, the capacity to learn, even the desire to live at all seem to be profoundly dependent on mothering behavior. Infants that are not sufficiently mothered have been seen to pine and die even when all other physical needs are met.

In the communal lifestyle of primitive society, the one absolutely indisputable possession was the infant that a mother produced from her own body. Indeed, the very spirit of motherhood was "mineness," *mamata,* according to early Hindus. On this spirit the clan system rested; mothers were the owners of their clans. One individual could partake of the life or property of another only through this mystic power of belonging.

As among animals, a human mother and her offspring also formed the one unbreakable bond that adult males might find incomprehensible, but with which no adult male dared interfere. The prohibition was of biological origin. A mother defending her young is still viewed as the most formidable power in the mammalian world; her ferocity can more than match a male's superior size or strength. Even in the Vedic pantheon, irresistible fighting spirit was symbolized by the Goddess as Durga the Inaccessible, Leader of the Mothers. No god or demon could stand against her. She was entirely indifferent to male defiance, appeal, or persuasion. Similar maternal warrior Goddesses appeared in pre-Hellenic matriarchies of Greece, Latium, and the Middle East: Artemis, Athene, Anath, Juno Martialis, Demeter Erinyes, Ma-Bellona, Ishtar the Lady of Victory, to name only a few.

Of course men prefer not to recognize such maternal power. They would rather view motherhood, even when symbolized by the Goddess, as entirely loving, giving, compliant, passively warm, and forever approachable—the infant's own wish-fulfilment image of the mother. But the ancients were realistic enough to perceive that Mother, even as Goddess, was quite capable of acting on her own and sweeping all resistance aside like chaff.

Even though the ancient powers of the Goddess are beginning to be recognized by modern scholars, patriarchal thinkers still hope to belittle the primacy of the maternal clan in social evolution. Some have claimed that matriarchal societies arose only with the development of agriculture, when gestation of the seed in Mother Earth was likened to pregnancy, and its germination to birth. But there is no real reason to think more primitive hunter-gatherer groups didn't also perceive motherhood as the essential beginning of their own lives. Such groups recently investigated have told of earlier ages when women were the rulers of their tribes, and the world's oldest religious artworks represent female fecundity only.

The helpless, immature human being was no less dependent on its mother before the rise of agricultural societies, no less grateful for the mother-given gift of life, no less in need of maternal training for acculturization and survival. And certainly women were no less clever, inventive, or assiduous in developing techniques and artifacts to improve the quality of life for their children and themselves. Though women and Goddesses are universally credited with the invention of agriculture, they are also seen as the originators of many other civilized pursuits: the manufacture of clothing, pottery, shelters, utensils, and tools; the domestication of animals; the development of decorative arts, music, alphabets, numbers, calendars, and other systems of calculation and record keeping. The contributions of men seem to have centered around the development of weapons and improved techniques of killing.

Men united in hunting groups, which gave them something useful to do while women were preoccupied with the important business of establishing the home nest or village, bearing and raising the next generation within its protective circle, and sharing new discoveries in the science of living. In such clan systems throughout most of humanity's existence on this earth, fatherhood was unknown, and the primary adult male kinsman was the maternal uncle, united with the mother by the all-important uterine blood bond. Each man's personal loyalty was to his mother's clan and his sisters' children. Sexual unions were casual, informal, and probably brief; they were not related to the true support system of the extended matrilineal family in which authority descended from mother to daughter.

That's why our conventional picture of the "caveman" defending "his" mate and "his" children is really quite absurd. No "caveman" knew he could beget children, any more than a male animal knows it; and it is highly unlikely that either he or his female counterpart had any interest in monogamy. Mothers and siblings were the true life companions of Stone Age people, along with the children (for women) or the nieces and nephews (for men). The nuclear family that we know today, consisting of father, mother, and their personal offspring, didn't exist.

Countless millenia were to pass before men's hunting groups developed enough confidence in their own killing power to challenge the creating power of the mothers. Eventually they would begin to claim their killing was as useful as women's birthing, planting, manufacturing, or building. Ritualization of killing gave it an enhanced importance, especially when the slain creature came to be regarded, by its killers, as a savior who willingly met death so others might live.

Primitive people everywhere tended to worship the animals they killed for food, to beg their forgiveness, or to render forgiveness unnecessary by pretending that death is no bad thing for the animal, for through its death it will become a divinity and a sacred ancestor of the tribe. When the animal's flesh and blood were consumed by the women, who subsequently brought forth children, the animal's spirit was said to live again in these children.

This was one of the primary sources of totemism, the primitive concept of animal ancestors. As Géza Roheim said, "Whatever is killed becomes father."[1] Since semen was not yet recognized as the vehicle of "seed," life-giving powers were attributed only to blood, after the manner of the female uterine blood bond.

Thus we find uncivilized hunting peoples—especially the men—making great ceremony with the animal they kill, propitiating it with reverent speeches, ornaments, offerings, and choice portions of the feast in which its own flesh is the main course. Similar principles applied to human sacrifices. Some of these, if not most, seem to have been quite willing to serve as sacrificial saviors for their people, motivated by a promise of postmortem godhood just as early Christian martyrs were motivated by a promise of instant glorification in heaven.

Human or animal, sacrificial victims were almost always male. Because they were not essential to the next generation, according to primitive thinking, males were expendable. Ancient Asiatic religious scriptures even made it a law, passed down by the gods themselves, that females must never be sacrificed.[2] As women were honored for courageously facing the dangers of childbirth, and for patiently accepting the extended responsibility of child care, so men were honored for facing death for the sake of others. In a sense, man's most ancient attempt to copy the sacred status of motherhood was the cult of the hero.

The savior-hero gave his lifeblood to Mother Earth as a fertility charm, to help replace the world's supply of life-giving blood produced by women. One of the oldest theories of the origin of life was, as the Bible puts it, "the blood is the life" (Deut. 12:23). As women were thought to create their own descendants from their own inner fountains, so men's earliest idea of taking part in the creative process was to contribute their own blood.

Among the oldest myths there is much evidence that formal sacrifices of males first arose from a misguided attempt to redesign male bodies to a female model, possibly in the hope of acquiring the female power of reproduction. Cutting off male genitals was constantly associated with fertility magic for ancient gods, in either human or animal form. The idea would have been to provide the male with a bleeding hole in crude imitation of a woman's body. Myths assumed the male deity could give birth successfully as a result of this treatment. Egypt's sun father Ra castrated himself to bring forth a new race from his genital blood.[3] The Hindu "Great God" had his penis removed, chopped up, and buried to bring forth a new generation.[4] A similar Babylonian god, Bel, mutilated his penis for blood that he could mingle with clay to produce people and animals, in imitation of the older Goddess Ninhursag, maker of life forms from the mixture of clay and menstrual blood.[5] A Mexican savior-deity, Quetzalcoatl, likewise gave blood from his sliced penis to the Earth Goddess's clay vessel, to repopulate the earth after the Deluge.[6] There were many such stories of castrated gods, even in classical Greco-Roman legends like those of Uranus, Adonis, and Attis. Even after human sacrifices were generally replaced by ritual killing of bulls, stags, rams, he-goats or stallions, it was customary to cut off the animals' genitalia.

The great mystery religions centered around ceremonies of blood because they were rooted in prehistoric matriarchy, with its proposition that blood was the real essence of life and creation. Even the name of Adam gave away the primal secret: it meant literally "man made of blood." The Goddess not only created the world out of her interior ocean of blood; she kept the very gods alive with periodic infusions of this magic elixir, which the Greeks described as Mother Hera's supernatural red wine.[7] As male gods gained prominence in the ancient pantheons, their worshipers continued to feed them meals of sacrificial blood. It was believed that this alone would propitiate them and bring about their forgiveness. According to the Hebrew God's version of the directive, "Without shedding of blood is no remission" (Heb. 9:22).

After the male role in reproduction was finally recognized, castration of men for religious reasons was gradually abandoned—with a few well-known exceptions, such as the priests of Attis and the early Christian castrati; also, men Jesus mentioned as having made themselves eunuchs for the sake of the kingdom of heaven (Matt. 19:12). Still, ceremonial imitations of castration remained in general use, on the theory that father gods required these offerings. Circumcision was the usual substitute. It has been shown that the blood of circumcision was deliberately intended to correspond to women's life-giving "moon-blood." In Egypt, boys were dressed as girls for their circumcision ceremonies.[8] In some primitive cultures even in the present century, it has been found that male genital mutilation (such as subincision) was referred to as "man's menstruation," the wound described as a vagina, and the whole purpose of the ceremony was said to unite each man with the spirit of the Mother.[9] Australian aborigines painted themselves and their sacred paraphernalia red for religious rites, declaring that the red color symbolized menstrual blood.[10] In southeastern Asia, the gods themselves derived their heavenly immortality from their intimate contact with the Great Mother's life-giving menstrual fluid.[11]

The original Crones of the matriarchal community were women past the age of menopause, in whom the blood of life no longer appeared outside the body. However, to our remote ancestors this was not necessarily a sign of its disappearance. It was clear enough that pregnant women also ceased to menstruate, presumably because their magic blood was otherwise occupied in the manufacture of the female miracle, a new life. When the aged mothers of the prehistoric tribe ceased to menstruate, it was similarly assumed that their magic blood was retained within the body for another wonderful purpose. Since it was usually described as wise blood, and old women were described as the wisest of mortals, it is not surprising to find that retained menstrual blood was often regarded as the source of their wisdom. The primitive idea was still extant even in Christian Europe up to the seventeenth century, when official opinions about witches included the assertion that their magic powers resulted from permanent retention of their lunar blood within their bodies.[12]

In the earliest times, old tribal mothers were credited with the important religious or magical lore, including the knowledge of right and wrong (or "good and evil") that led them to formulate laws and other rules of behavior. The so-called Tablets of Law that the biblical Moses received from his mountain god were later copies of much earlier tablets of law received from the Goddess herself. Mother Tiamat, for example, gave her sacred tablets to her first son, the god Kingu, whose blood helped contribute life-giving waters to the newly created earth, and formed the first man, according to some accounts.[13] Cretan Mother Rhea gave her tablets of law to the first King Minos on Mount Dicte, the location of her uterine cave temple, where she gave birth to gods. The wisdom of Maat (Mother) determined the rules of truth and justice in ancient

Egypt; and it was she who determined an Egyptian's ultimate fate by weighing his soul in her balances after death. Roman lawgivers spoke of the great Earth Mother as Ceres Legifera, "Ceres the Lawgiver;" their *ius naturale* or "natural law" was the legal system of the pre-Roman matriarchate.[14] As mothers made the rules for their children's instruction, safety, and socialization, so the ancient tribal mothers made the rules to guide the behavior of all. This matriarchal clan system has been called "by far the most successful form that human association has assumed."[15] One reason for its success may well have been that its laws were made chiefly by women, whose quicker awareness of connections and relationships would have made them fairer lawmakers than men. Carol Gilligan says, "The discovery now being celebrated by men in mid-life of the importance of intimacy, relationships, and care is something that women have known from the beginning. . . . In the different voice of women lies the truth of an ethic of care, the tie between relationship and responsibility, and the origins of aggression in the failure of connection."[16]

Images of the tribal Mother or Goddess-Queen may be found in most ancient literature. Discernment in dispensing justice is often her outstanding attribute. As the Bible says of the virtuous matriarch, "She openeth her mouth with wisdom; and in her tongue is the law of kindness" (Prov. 31:26). The *Epic of Gilgamesh* presents Mother Ninsun, a demigoddess-matriarch "Who Knew All Wisdom," foundress of the third dynasty of Ur, 2112-2095 B.C. She was said to have mothered many kings and legendary heroes.[17]

There is some evidence that the tribal grandmothers of prehistory were the originators of law. Even misogynist Greeks and Romans of the classical period attributed the foundations of their law codes to various forms of the ancestral Mother Goddess: Demeter, or Ceres. In Egypt, the name of one of the oldest Goddesses, Heqit or Hekat, was formed from the root *heq*, "intelligence," which also meant a tribal ruler in the predynastic period.[18] Greeks called this deity Hecate, making her the Crone form of the Mother of the Gods (Hera), and establishing her in the underworld as Queen of the Shades, an alter ego of Persephone. Later, Christian authorities made her Queen of Witches. But Egyptians assimilated her to the Divine Grandmother bearing the flail, symbol of authority.[19] She was the source of *hekau*, the "words of power" that commanded and decided all things, including forces of creation and destruction.

Ancient Egyptians usually regarded the mother, not the father, as the most important member of a household. In common with most other contemporary inhabitants of the Eurasian land mass, they traced their descent through mothers and regarded women as founders of families.[20] As leaders of relationship groups united by the all-important blood bond, elder women naturally made the rules for such groups. Their codices, attributed to the *heq* of tribal mothers, came down to dynastic times as the Laws of Maa, or Maat: alternative names for the Goddess as Mother of Truth.

Even the gods were constrained to live by the Laws of Maat, which were largely benevolent and pacifist, foreshadowing by many centuries the "golden rule" that appeared later in Buddhist, Jewish, and Christian tradition. Some of Maat's laws commanded that no one should cause pain to others, nor make anyone sorrowful, nor steal, cheat, bear false witness, stir up strife; neither should anyone harm animals, damage fertile land, or befoul waters—precepts that our own civilization would have done well to heed, before it became too late.[21]

Conservation of natural resources was an important part of matriarchal morality, which usually taught that the Great Mother (Nature) would provide adequate sustenance for all her children, as long as no one became greedy for more than a fair share. Communal ownership of goods and resources was characteristic of prepatriarchal societies, whereas overproduction, hoarding, and accumulation of wealth in the hands of an aristocratic class seem to have typified established patriarchies.

A combination of Hekat and Maa as Hek-Maa, "Maternal Wisdom," may have been the origin of Hebrew Hokmah, which also meant "Maternal Wisdom," the spirit appearing in Proverbs 8 as God's cocreator. Greek translators of the Bible rendered her name as Sophia, "Wisdom." Christian interpreters pretended that she was only a semiabstract personification of God's wisdom, though the Bible itself contradicts this theory in Proverbs 9, where the Goddess Hokmah (or Sophia) is ridiculed along with her priestesses, her seven-pillared temples, and her sacramental meals of wine and meat, partakers of which were consigned to hell by the biblical writer.

Yet, in the *Wisdom of Solomon,* Hokmah was equated with the Egyptian Goddess and called the all-powerful Mother and Artificer of all things, a spirit penetrating all creation, higher than the stars, fairer than sunlight.[22] The Gnostic gospel *On the Origin of the World* said it was she who gave birth to Jehovah himself, and taught him how to create the forms of living creatures, though she alone infused them with the power of life.[23]

Scriptures hinting at feminine primacy or power were eliminated from the canon, and later male scholars tended to overlook the few remaining allusions to an early matriarchate, such as the period when women "judged" all Israel (Judg. 4), or the statement that the owners of houses were mothers, not fathers (Ruth 1:8). Sometimes the words translated as "God" in the English Bible were actually feminine plurals in the original language, or the Hebrew plural *elohim,* meaning not "God" but "goddesses-and-gods."

The Bible itself was named after Byblos, one of the Great Mother's oldest sacred cities, where her priestesses kept a great library of papyrus scrolls that the Greeks called *byblos* (bibles).[24]

Many fairly obscure words bear witness to male scholars' tendency to stretch translations into a patriarchal Procrustean bed. An old Icelandic title of the supreme justice of the intertribal council, *Lögsögomathr,* has been rendered "Lawspeaker"—despite its literal meaning, "Mother-Who-Speaks-the-Word-of-the-Law."[25]

Similarly, the word *saga* has been translated out of its original meaning, "She-Who-Speaks," that is, an oracular priestess, such as were formerly associated with sacred poetry. The literal meaning of *saga* was "female sage." It was also one of the names of the Scandinavian Great Goddess.[26] The written sagas of Scandinavia were originally sacred histories kept by female *sagas* or "sayers," who knew how to write them in runic script. Among northern tribes, men were usually illiterate. Writing and reading the runes were female occupations.[27] Consequently, runes were associated with witchcraft by medieval Christian authorities, who distrusted all women's lore. To them, *saga* became a synonym for *witch.* [28]

Another word for sacred poetry preserved by northern priestesses was *Edda,* originally a name of the primal "Great-Grandmother," also rendered Erda, Ertha, Urd, or Earth.[29] She was invoked by every singer of sagas. A formal invocation of Erda as the Muse appears at the beginning of the *Nibelungenlied.* According to old ballads gathered from the bards of northern Europe, in ancient times men could not perform sacred poetry, invocations, or any form of magic unless they were educated and directed by women.[30]

Magic, prophecy, healing, fertility, birth, death, seasonal ceremonies, and sacred literature were largely the province of women in pre-Christian Europe. During centuries of patriarchal conquest, new laws were set against the old systems of mother-right and matrilineal property inheritance, to take property away from the female family heads recognized by paganism, and place it in the hands of men, according to the church's ideas of father-right. Predictably, women often refused to abandon the older customs, which had given them spiritual, economic, and social prominence. Many of them realized that the church sought to reduce women's significance, to mock their sacred songs and stories as "old wives' tales," to diabolize their deities, to condemn their magic, even to blame them for all the world's sins.

Eventually, Christianity broke the back of the female-centered tribal system. Early missionaries to the British Isles wrote of the "great sin" prevalent among the natives: They paid no attention to fatherhood. Sons didn't respect their fathers.[31] They revered their mothers, grandmothers, and maternal uncles. The matrilineal system was so ingrained that missionaries had to call Christ "our sister's son," because that was the honorable male relationship the people understood.[32] This "great sin" was later corrected by a religion that attributed divinity only to a Father and a Son, denying the divinity of the Mother, even though she was officially described as the parent of both (Mother of Christ, Mother of God, bride of her own offspring).

Among numerous other formerly respectable words for a wisewoman was *hag,* which also became a pejorative synonym for *witch.* *Hag* used to mean "a holy one," from Greek *hagia,* as in hagiolatry, worship of saints. Possibly this too was related to Egyptian *heq.*

During the Middle Ages, when women still practiced the "fairy religion," *hag* was said to mean the same as *fairy.*[33] In Old High German, *Hagazussa* meant a priestess of the underground mother Hel, or her Grandmother transformation, Angurboda, sometimes called Hag of the Iron Wood.[34] Angurboda also mothered the wolfish psychopomps (soul-carriers) northern tribesmen called Moon-dogs, who carried away the dead to their appointed places in the afterworld.[35]

The Hag was worshiped as a Goddess by Saxons and Danes in the form of an aniconic stone idol, probably similar to the stone embodying the Great Mother of the Gods (Cybele) in pagan Rome. The sacred stone of Scone seems to have been such an idol. It used to be called the Hag of Scone. Medieval legend said this Hag was once the leader of an Elf tribe (that is, a heathen Goddess). She was turned into stone by the curse of a Christian missionary.[36]

Despite the legendary curse, the festival of the Hag continued to be celebrated each New Year's Eve in Britain, up to the nineteenth century. Known as the Hagmenai (Hag's Moon), the ceremony involved folk gathering together around a fire after midnight, exchanging the kiss of peace with one another, and giving blessings and good wishes for the New Year. Contemporary clergymen said, however, that this custom meant an invocation of the devil.[37]

The stone of Scone, erstwhile Hag, still occupies an important ceremonial position in modern Britain. It (or she) rests beneath the coronation throne in Westminster Abbey, being considered essential to the crowning of every monarch. Therefore, in a way the stone recalls the heathen custom whereby kings and chieftains were chosen by tribal councils of old women, and inaugurated over sacred stones, which were said to speak aloud, signifying divine acceptance of each new ruler.

Just as it was customary among American Indians for councils of elder women to choose the sachems (chiefs), so it was customary among Picts, Gaels, Teutons, Celts, Galatians, Lydians, Scythians, Sumerians, Akkadians, and other ancient peoples for councils of elder women to choose the kings and war leaders.[38] Often, male rulers were selected only from certain matrilineal bloodlines, subject to approval by the queen, who represented the Goddess of the land.[39] Early Babylonian and Assyrian kings specifically announced in their coronation hymns that they were chosen for their office by the Goddess herself, married to her, crowned by her, or created by her hands.[40]

The tradition of speaking stones, used to announce acceptance of the ruler, is found especially in lands colonized by Celtic tribes, who regarded the stone as the oracle of Mother Earth, and would not obey a candidate she refused.[41] Among these magic stones one might number the famous speaking stone at Blarney Castle, now said to bestow the gift of speech, and the equally famous sword stone that gave King Arthur his magic weapon at the New Year, thus declaring his right to the throne.

The shadowy myth of the king-choosing Hag stone left some of its most intriguing traces at Mecca, now the center of the world's most male-dominant religion, Islam. Each year, countless pilgrims go to Mecca to worship, in the name of Allah, the famous Black Stone of the Kaaba (Cube), which was actually a sacred object of pilgrimage long before the establishment of Islam. The Black Stone was holy when Arabia was inhabited by matriarchal tribes, ruled by queens, and devoted to another version of the Mother Goddess.

Prominent among pre-Islamic tribes of Arabia were the Koreshites, children of the Goddess Kore, or Q're, Mohammed's own ancestors, residents of Mecca. Members of this tribe were hereditary guardians of the sacred Black Stone. The deity they worshiped was sometimes known as the Old Woman. Her Black Stone was marked by a female genital sign, and covered by a veil—like the Crone appearing as Mother of Destiny, representing the veiled future.[42] Later, male priests usurped the functions of the priestesses, but continued to call themselves Beni Shaybah, "Sons of the Old Woman."[43]

Worshipers of Kore or Q're were the original authors of the oldest sections of the Koran. Even Muslims admit this work existed many centuries before the time of Mohammed. Legend said it was copied from a divine prototype that appeared in heaven at the beginning of eternity, the Preserved Tablet, or Mother of the Book.[44] Reminiscent of other, older versions of the Goddess's Tablets of Destiny, this literary Mother was written down by holy *imams* or "wise ones," a word related to Semitic *ima,* "mother."[45]

For more than a thousand years of recorded history before the advent of Islam, Arabia had a matriarchal culture, governed by a series of divinely appointed queens.[46] Primary Goddess of the country was a trinity of the Virgin (Kore), the Powerful One (Al-Uzza), and the Moon, Manat, whose name is still synonymous with

Destiny or Fate in Arabic. Sometimes the Goddess was called Al-Lat, the earlier feminine form of Allah.

Islamic tradition says Mohammed once prostrated himself in adoration of the Goddess, and joined in reverent praise of her with his fellow Meccans, one of whom remarked sarcastically that Ibn Abi Kabshah (Mohammed's matrilineal name) had finally said something good about feminine divinity. Later interpreters treated Mohammed's slip into Goddess worship as a temporary lapse brought about by Satan.[47]

The Black Stone of the Kaaba, revered then and now as Arabia's most sacred object, may be likened to the black stone representing the Goddess Artemis at her Amazonian shrine of Themiscyra, or the black stone representing the Goddess Cybele in Phrygia and Rome. Variations of Cybele's name—Kubaba, Kuba, Kube—have been linguistically linked with the Kaaba.[48] Such black stones were evidently meteorites, believed to have been sent down from the Queen of Heaven as special gifts to her people.[49]

In Rome, as in her earlier shrine at Pessinus, Cybele's black stone was ceremonially fructified with blood from the severed genitals of her self-castrated priests, during the celebration of the death and resurrection of her son-lover Attis, who also castrated himself, and perished in donating his blood to his Mother Earth.[50] The blood rite signifies a religion of extreme antiquity, predating the discovery of fatherhood. The aniconic stone stood for the Goddess's Crone phase in particular, as the Old Woman governing the mysteries of death and rebirth.

Pre-Islamic Mecca apparently entertained similar ideas of its Goddess. Modern Muslims still carry on the solemn veiling of the Black Stone under its embroidered *kiswa,* which covers the entire cubical shrine of the Kaaba (about forty feet on a side). Veiling of the Crone stone was a common custom of ancient Goddess worship. In her trinity of past, present, and future, the future figure was veiled because one look at her might mean sudden premature death.

Since the Crone *was* death, one could see her "face to face" only in one's final moments of life. The inscription on the Goddess's temple at Sais said (in words later copied into the biblical Book of Revelation): "I am all that has been, that is, and that will be. No mortal has yet been able to lift the veil that covers me."[51] When a man saw what was behind her veil, he was no longer mortal.

Many myths present the idea that the Crone could kill with a straight look from her unveiled eye. It was a logical corollary to the theory that she revealed the mystery of herself only to the dying. Perhaps the best known of these evil-eye myths was that of Medusa, third of the trinity of Gorgons, whose petrifying look may have symbolized the "turning to stone" of the dead, in the form of a grave pillar, or funerary portrait statue.

Most people are familiar with the classic tale of Perseus killing Medusa with a backward stroke of his sword, by looking only at her reflection in the mirror of his polished shield, then carrying her severed head back to his municipal Goddess, Athene, who placed it on her aegis (breastplate). This tale was told in Athens to account for the traditional appearance of Medusa's snake-haired head on the holy aegis. An in-depth analysis of the myth shows that the Medusa head symbolized female wisdom—said to be Athene's outstanding characteristic—and that it had appeared as one of Athene's attributes long before she was adopted by patriarchal Athenians and reinterpreted as the Wisdom of Father Zeus, born full-armed from his brain.

Medusa was a variant of the Greek name for Athene's mythological mother, Metis, whom Zeus supposedly swallowed while she was pregnant with Athene, in a naive myth invented to account for his subsequent improbable pregnancy. Like Medusa, Metis meant "female wisdom." She represented Zeus's claim to omniscience, as the Gnostic Sophia later represented God's. Athene was originally the Virgin aspect of her trinity. Instead of springing from Zeus's head as the later myths claimed, Athene was born in Libya at Tritonis, "the Place of Three Queens." Some called her Libyan mother Tritone, "the Third Queen," probably the wise Crone member of the trinity.[52]

Worship of snakes as embodiments of divine female wisdom characterized the matriarchal people Herodotus called the Libyan Amazons.[53] A female face surrounded by serpent-hair meant menstrual mysteries and the wisdom of the Crone, appearing as such on prophylactic ceremonial masks. Argives called the Gorgon Medusa a Libyan queen slain in battle by their hero Perseus, who brought back either her head or her taboo mask.[54] It could have been a portion of her holy image.

Gorgon was a name of Athene herself, in her Destroyer aspect.[55] Neith, Ath-enna, Anath, and Medusa were various names for the Triple Goddess in Phoenician Libya. Far from attributing her birth to a male god, the Egyptians said her name meant "I have come from myself."[56]

The Gorgon's evil eye was attributed to many other manifestations of the Crone, pointing to a broad dissemination of the idea that to see her face to face was to die. As a postmortem judge, she was usually credited with a piercing gaze from which nothing could be hidden. Her Egyptian name as Mother of Truth and Justice, Maat, derived from the universal mother-syllable Maa (Ma). In Egypt this also meant "to see," and it was shown in hieroglyphics as an eye.[57]

In the Middle East, the Crone had several manifestations as an all-seeing eye, notably the huge-eyed Syrian Goddess Mari who could search men's souls.[58] As Anath or Anat, the all-seeing Crone reappeared in early Christian legend under the name of Aynat, the Evil Eye of the Earth. Abyssinian Christians called her an old witch and claimed Jesus commanded that she must be burned and her ashes scattered to the winds to prevent her resurrection.[59]

It was a common conviction among Christians everywhere that old witches had the evil eye. Muslims were similarly convinced, even going so far as to attribute the evil eye to every post-menopausal woman, witch or not. Up to the nineteenth century, no old woman was allowed to attend public appearances of the Shah of Iran, because her look was considered dangerous to his divine person.[60]

Certainly a major influence on such fears was an unconscious survival of the prepatriarchal view of the clan grandmother as a repository of magical wisdom, discernment, and the ability to invoke the curse of death, because of her mysterious relationship to the Goddess-as-Crone. To look through the veil that hid future events was the function of any seeress, and any postmenopausal woman was believed to have some degree of this foresight. There was never any clear distinction between foreseeing a fatal event, and bringing it about by the very process of foretelling it.

In practice, to cast a death spell was often no more than to describe the death in sufficiently minute detail, in a prophetic style of utterance. Therefore, during witch persecutions, old women who both stared and mumbled were particularly suspect. They were also feared. Officers of the Inquisition forced accused witches to enter the court backward, so they couldn't have the advantage of a first glance at their judges, which might place the latter under the power of the evil eye. It was almost as if the church might have remembered the altar dedicated to the evil eye in pre-Christian Rome, on the Esquiline, where the third of the three fortune goddesses bore the name of Mala Fortuna, bringer of doom.[61]

Despite extensive diabolization of Crone figures both mortal and divine, there were curious survivals in patriarchy of the wise Crone as a divinity essential to, and perhaps more powerful than, God—like Athene in her role of the Wisdom of Zeus, and her Roman counterpart Minerva as the Wisdom of Jupiter. Throughout Indo-European religions it was a common belief that a god would be powerless without the guidance of a feminine embodiment of wisdom.

In India this feminine wisdom figure was usually called Shakti, an almost untranslatable amalgam of wife, mistress, queen, power, genius, strength, authority, mind, vulva, woman, and cosmic energy.[62] Each god needed his own Shakti. Without her, he couldn't act at all. Women were called shaktis on earth. The Great Goddess was a Great Shakti, representing all the world's power-to-act.[63]

There is considerable evidence that this concept was not unknown to followers of father gods in the West, even the most patriarchal of them, including the Judeo-Christian deity. Among early Christian Gnostics there was even a system called *synesaktism,* literally "the Way of Shaktism," which the orthodox church officially suppressed before the seventh century, although it kept recurring in various forms throughout European history.[64]

The usual Gnostic name for the Wisdom Goddess was Sophia, said to be the creatress, or else the preexisting Mother of God the Creator. A Gnostic gospel called the *Apocryphon of John,* still in active use during the eighth century A.D., stated that Sophia made the God who made the world.[65] He was an ignorant God, forgetting his mother Sophia who brought him into being and suffused him with her creative energy and ideas. So he began to claim that he was the sole creator, and Sophia was obliged to punish him for his arrogance.[66]

Gnostic scriptures also suggested that the feminine principle of wisdom was embodied in Eve, whom the Bible called Mother of All Living; she was Sophia's Logos "made flesh." As in the Gorgon symbol, Eve's feminine Wisdom was linked with the serpent. Words for *Eve, instruction,* and *serpent* are closely allied in Aramaic: *Hawah, hawa, hewya.* The *Hypostasis of the Archons* said the Female Spiritual Principle was part of both Eve and the serpent, who taught man the all-important knowledge of good and evil, without which he could never hope to achieve heaven.[67] According to even the canonical Bible story, God forbade both the fruit of the tree of knowledge and the fruit of the tree of life, wishing to keep both wisdom and immortality away from humans. Therefore, some Gnostics revered the serpent and Eve as the true liberators of humanity.

On the Origin of the World said an evil deity lied to Adam, calling himself one of the rulers of heaven, saying Eve was not the life-giving incarnation of Sophia, but rather a product of Adam's own rib. Sophia cursed this evil deity and cast him down from heaven. With others of his kind, he was fated to be destroyed at doomsday, when Sophia would "drive out the gods of Chaos whom she created together with the first Father. . . . They will be wiped out by their own injustice."[68]

Obviously, Gnostic scriptures had a different slant on the creation story from the one that became canonical, which left out the female principle, trivialized Eve, and diabolized her serpent. Orthodox Christians collected and burned many copies of the two or three hundred different alternative gospels extant in the fourth and fifth centuries A.D. Nevertheless, some of the feminine imagery for God's wisdom survived in various forms, including that of the female dove (symbol of Aphrodite) taken to represent the Holy Ghost, otherwise known as Hagia Sophia (Holy Female Wisdom). Mandaean Christians gave the Holy Ghost the female name of Ruha, "Spirit," calling her the mother of the seven planetary archons.[69]

Despite systematic destruction of books describing the Wise Goddess as God's all-important Mother or spouse, some scholars and mystics kept reviving her at intervals through the Middle Ages, distinguishing between this primal female power and God's accepted Mother-bride, Mary. A fourteenth-century translator of pseudo-Dionysius said God's consort was the "unbegun and everlasting Wisdom . . . the sovereign-substantial Firsthood, the sovereign Goddess, and the sovereign Good."[70]

The *Book of the Secrets of Enoch* carried into medieval times one of the early Gnostic accounts of the creation that contradicted the canonical one from Genesis. This account said it was not God but the Wise Goddess, Sophia/Hokmah, who created man from the seven "consistencies": his flesh from earth, blood from dew, eyes from sunlight, bones from stone, intelligence from cloud, veins and hair from grass, soul from the wind. This gave man his "seven natures," corresponding to the seven souls supposedly given each human being by the Goddess in Egypt, under the names of Isis, Hathor, or Hek-Maa, who corresponded to the Hebrew Hokmah.[71] The Alexandrian philosopher Philo the Jew, who died about 40 A.D., stated unequivocally that this same Wise Goddess was the wife of God. In the third century A.D., rabbinical writings described her as the admonisher of God. She scolded him for his excessive vengefulness.[72]

By the sixteenth century, the Wise Goddess had acquired the Latin name of Sapientia (Wisdom), and was described as the being, light, and life of all things. As a trinity, Divine Providence, she consisted of Sapientia *creans,* the Creatress; Sapientia *disponans,* the Disposer; and Sapientia *gubernans,* the Ruler. This was not far from the Oriental female trinity of Creator, Preserver, Destroyer. Edmund Spenser called this Sapientia the "sovereign darling of the Deity," enthroned in his bosom, and "clad like a Queen in royal robes."[73]

The Renaissance brought a new influx of Oriental ideas into Europe, including several time-honored images of the Goddess as a universal soul or mind. Jewish Cabalists incorporated some of these images into their doctrine of the lost Shekina (Shakti), God's former spouse, whose disappearance had brought on all the evil in the world. Cabalistic philosophers held that all wrongs could be righted and all troubles healed if only God and his lost spouse could be reunited. Among Cabalists there was also a revival of the early Jewish-Gnostic belief that all the world's soul—that is, life-giving, motivating spirit—originated with the female Shekinas who were emanations of the primordial Great Wisdom.[74]

The Shekinas undoubtedly began as divinized tribal ancestresses during Israel's matriarchal period, when the same primordial Great Wisdom was incarnated as Sarah in the time of Abraham, as Rebekah in the time of Isaac, and as Rachel in the time of Jacob, according to the tradition preserved by Joseph Gikatilla.[75] Such incarnations of the Goddess corresponded to the Hittite matriarchs known as "elderly women," who guided the decisions of government and were associated with prophecy and healing.[76]

Like other ancestral deities, the Shekinas merged into *the* Shekina, whose splendor created and fed the angels, Talmudic literature said. Yet, even the angels must cover their faces before her unbearable radiance, and her body stretches millions of miles in extent.[77]

The important point about the Shekina was that she embodied God's power and intelligence. Without her, he would be unable to act at all. This was a common feature of ancient religions. It must be remembered that without their Shaktis, Hindu gods were thought unable to move, think, function, or create.[78] The similar female Wisdom-consort of Greek father god Zeus, Metis (or Medusa), "Wisdom," true mother of Athene, also embodied the divine mind. Athene's alleged birth from Zeus's head was a patriarchal reinterpretation of the ancient iconography: the feminine image of power-to-act emanating from the god, after she energized him.

Her Latin name, Minerva, stemmed from the Etruscan Goddess Menarva, a similar source of lunar wisdom or mind *(mens)*, whose spirit empowered the gods. As in the cult of Athene, Anath, Lilith, and other Middle Eastern versions of the same Goddess, her totem was the wise owl, still half-playfully depicted every Halloween as the companion of witches.[79] Hence, the owl was a bird of enlightenment, as in the expression "a little bird told me." It was said a sage could understand the bird's language after the sacred serpents of the Wise Goddess, Metis-Medusa, had licked his ears. This sequence of events is still found in many fairy tales.

The basic idea of the god's indispensable female power source applied equally to central Asian shamans and other spiritual authorities on earth, including Hindu, Jewish, and Roman priests, who had to be married in order to become priests at all. The municipal high priest of Rome was forbidden to occupy his holy office unless he remained married to the high priestess of Juno, whose name was another word for every woman's soul.[80] Each woman had a *juno* as each man had a *genius* (spirit).

It used to be thought that every man needed his own embodiment of the Goddess—Shakti, Shekina, Sophia, Juno, Anima, Psyche, Sapientia, and so on—the Muse who gave him understanding and spiritual power. Priests especially needed such power, otherwise their magic would be ineffectual and their rituals worthless. It was believed that deities wouldn't listen to the invocations, prayers, mantras, spells, exorcisms, or sacramental recitations of a priest who had no spouse.

Since all gods are basically projections of their priests' own personalities, dreams, and wishes, it was only natural that both priests and gods would require spouses in the time when men still thought their only true connection with the universal life force lay through intimate relationship with a woman.

In prehistoric ages, women embodied the earth and owned the real estate, as well as holding within themselves the "wise blood" that formed life in the matrilineal clan system. Therefore, men's only connection with the life-sustaining earth was through marriage. Also, man's spiritual energy was supposed to need periodic refreshment by contact with its true fount within a female body. Similarly, gods were considered helpless without their sexual partners, who were simultaneously their Divine Mothers, providing life and mind to each god in both his father and son phases.

This became a hidden tenet of Western religion, mostly suppressed, but popping up here and there in esoteric or heretical systems such as Manichaeism and the Cabala, which were influenced by Tantric Goddess worship. It was the idea most feared by the wholly masculine church, which had struggled from its inception to become the only repository of learning and the only legitimate source of wisdom. To this end, the early church burned thousands of books and closed any schools that taught alternative modes of thought. Most of all, early churchmen never ceased to denigrate the mental and moral qualities of women, and to diabolize their Goddess. Gnostic scriptures that emphasized female preeminence in wisdom were among the first committed to the fire.

We know of at least two books about the wise All-Mother of humanity, every copy of which met destruction, only their titles remaining in other works: *The First Book of Noraia* and *The First Logos of Noraia,* said to contain female "names of power." Noraia or Norea was mentioned by the Gnostics as Eve's only daughter, sister-wife of Seth, therefore the universal mother of the human race. She was "pure in character and exalted in knowledge."[81] Little more is known of this primal matriarch. The canonical Bible mentions only Eve and her three sons, Cain, the deceased Abel, and Seth who replaced him. As far as the Bible is concerned, one might think the human race continued to reproduce without benefit of wombs.

Wherever references to the primal Goddess couldn't be diabolized, masculinized, or quietly dropped, early churchmen tended to convert them into mythical saints. Since Europeans persisted in attending the same old pagan shrines even after nominal conversion to Christianity, often the church's only recourse was to canonize the local native deity as a long-ago martyr, and supply some new relics to replace the ancient idol.

A well-known example of the Wise Mother converted by this method was Saint Brigit, former Virgin-Mother-Crone trinity of the Celtic Brigantian empire. Her shrine at Kildare, maintained by her sacred women, was taken over and made into a convent. Saint Brigit was said to have taught men the same arts originally attributed to the Goddess Brigit: midwifery, medicine, smith craft.

So eager were monkish scribes to Christianize Brigit that, in the confusion, they called her the bride of Saint Patrick, the Goidelic Mary, Prophetess of Christ, Queen of Heaven, and even Mother of Jesus.[82] The ninth-century Cormac's Glossary more correctly called her a trinity of three sisters, all named Brigit, collectively "the female sage, or woman of wisdom—that is, Brigit the Goddess, whom poets adored."[83]

Brigit's Crone form, Cerridwen, particularly embodied the wisdom that inspired poets. She also represented death. Like her Syrian counterpart Astarte and her Greek counterpart Demeter-Persephone (Demeter the Destroyer), she appeared totemically as a white sow. This and other manifestations of the Crone-as-sow probably descended from the Diamond Sow of Southeast Asia, regarded even in modern times as an incarnation of the Queen of Heaven.[84] Welsh monastic tradition said a mystic white sow told such saints as Dyfrig, Kentigern, Cadog, and Brynach where to establish their monasteries. In Pembrokeshire, a famous Druidic cromlech still marks the site of what used to be an enclosed chamber, known as the Womb of Cerridwen, where would-be sages probably "incubated" in order to receive their enlightenment.[85]

Concerning ancient traditions that persistently link poetic inspiration, literary accomplishment, and civilized arts with the Crone figure, it must be kept in mind that—contrary to Christians' poor opinion of female mentality—pagans viewed women as the wiser sex, and the Wise Goddess as the ultimate source of truth. Tantric lore credited the Goddess with the invention of all logical systems of measurement and mathematics (that is, "mother-wisdom"), as well as astronomy, music, calendars, and alphabets. Isis was said to have given the hieroglyphic alphabet to the Egyptians and, under her Libyan name of Metis-Medusa, the Greek alphabet to Heracles. Pythagoras first learned ancient alphabets from the priestesses of Crete, then visited the Hyperborean school in Cornwall to study letters, astronomy, and science under the British Goddess-Queen Samothea, or Death Goddess, a common appellation of the Crone.[86]

An important point about these traditions of the knowledge-giving, civilization-creating Crone is that her intellectual gifts were not based solely on what is now called "feminine intuition," emotion, or unconscious responses. She was equally credited with analytical intelligence of the sort that has become stereotyped as "masculine." Her wisdom was both broader and deeper than that of the gods. She could think more clearly than they, as well as more empathetically. In the currently popular metaphor of the bipolar brain, she represented neither "left-brain" nor "right-brain" thinking exclusively, but a more efficient use of both.

A few brave souls in the modern era (such as H. L. Mencken) have gone so far as to define that wonderfully indefinable quality of "feminine intuition" in a way that most men would rather not have it defined: as superior intelligence, compounded of keener senses, more acute powers of observation, quicker analysis, and perhaps better memory. When girls exhibit these qualities in school, showing themselves better students than the boys, patriarchal culture tends to label them more docile or more trainable, rather than more intelligent.

However, it is time to consider the possibility that females may have a statistically verifiable advantage over males in general mental acuity. This would not be inconsistent with nature's requirement for quick wits in the sex responsible for continuity of the race, in any species. By contrast to males, females must care for more individuals than themselves, and their attention must never lapse while their young are dependent. It would not be surprising, therefore, to find that females have a somewhat greater capacity to perceive, think, and react appropriately to stimuli. Elder females would inevitably add to their innate abilities the conclusions drawn from their experience of life.

In human patriarchal societies, by the mere fact of having lived to old age in a "man's world," most elder women would have learned things about men that few men would want openly discussed. Frequently, men seem panicked by the idea that women may have seen through their disguises and understood their weaknesses. The ancient figure of the elder woman as judge may be interpreted as a threat, due to male fears of being judged too harshly, of being unable to "measure up," of being reduced again to the terrified little boy before the stern eye of a disapproving mother. Hence the widespread male fear of the old woman's level look, her all-seeing "evil eye."

In reality, however, it is usually not the mothers but the fathers who impose the harshest standards, introduce hierarchical patterns, and instill lifelong fears of not measuring up—in every matter from simple physical dimensions, like penis size or body height, to the size of scores, salaries, properties, and political influence. Men automatically judge and classify each other in every walk of life: education, sport, business, the military, politics, even the conspicuously male-dominated world of organized crime.

Patriarchal religion follows the same pattern. Never was there such an implacable judge as the Judeo-Christian God, declaring all human beings sinful by the mere fact of being born, and condemning nearly all of them to eternal punishment as horrible as the most sadistic imagination could envision. God's spokesmen maintained that the vast majority of his "children" would spend eternity in the flames of hell, despite the torture already inflicted on the Son, which was supposed to have satisfied the Father enough to soften his heart toward the rest of his wretched dependents.[87] As Robert

Ingersoll succinctly said, "God so loved the world that he made up his mind to damn a large majority of the human race."[88]

Actually, the very concept of human beings as God's "children" was a leftover from a matriarchal age. The biblical God had no children. He was not a begetting father, but a manufacturer. The Bible story said people were not his offspring, but his handmade products.

On the other hand, the Goddess was always regarded as a mother who had, at some time, given birth to the world's living creatures, and remained directly, personally, and intimately involved with them. The power of the governing matriarch was only an extension into adult life of a mother's natural authority over dependent children. Even as the death-dealing Crone she acted directly and personally. Her worshipers never evolved such a heavenly hierarchy as the bureaucratic Christian chain of command with God at the top of the pyramid, approachable only through a series of intercessors: deacons, priests, bishops, archbishops, cardinals, popes, saints, angels, archangels, Principalities, Powers, Virtues, Dominions, Thrones, Cherubim, Seraphim, and finally his Son or else his (officially nondivine) Mother-bride. Man created his political heaven to match his political earth.

Whether or not he sat enthroned at the top of this chain of command, like the president of a vast corporation, this particular God had no existence in human minds until a late period of history. Humanity's more remote ancestors knew only one source of life: Mother.

The first threat to the long age of the maternal clan arose when men began to understand that males had something to do with reproduction, and that it was not only the hidden wisdom of the female that had discovered the mystery of bringing forth life. Man probably didn't find this out for himself. It is more likely that he was instructed by woman, traditional keeper of dates and seasons, inventor of calendars based on her own biological rhythms, undoubtedly the first to discover a connection between sexual intercourse and birth through her formal methods of recording time. Adrienne Rich says, "It is not from God the Father that we derive the idea of paternal authority; it is out of the struggle for paternal control of the family that God the Father is created."[89]

The wisdom attributed to God the Father was also preempted

from earlier matricentric Goddess worship by rather crude mythological revisions. Like an earthly king, God owed his quality of wisdom to some connection with the Wise Goddess, even though the connection may have been deliberately written out of the script by his later priesthoods.

Rightly styled the Thousand-Named Goddess, she might appear as Tiamat, Maat, Metis, Medusa, Manat, Hokmah, Hekat, Kore, Ceres, Cybele, Saga, Sophia, Sapientia, Isis, Shekina, Shakti, Athene, Aphrodite, Fortuna, Tritone, Demeter, Ninsun, Neith, Rhea, Ruha, Al-Uzza, Brigit, Noraia, Lilith, Eve, Sarasvati, Kali, or under any of several hundred other names. Each tribe and nationlet had its own set of names for her. When small groups merged with larger groups, various titles of the Goddess came together and were used more or less interchangeably.

Pantheons of different goddesses were sometimes created from this circumstance and assigned to different departments in patriarchal style. However, upon closer inspection, the characteristics of all the departmentalized goddesses tended to merge. One of the most remarkable things about the Great Mother was the uniformity of her images around the world. From China to Celtic Britain, from the Indian Ocean to the North Sea, she was essentially one.

Her temples were everywhere. She was once revered by every human being born of woman—which meant, of course, every human being, period. Until the advent of the present comparatively short historical era, never before, in his several million years on earth, did man undertake to erase a whole archetypal concept common to his entire species. Now it has been done, and the shrines of the Goddess have almost completely disappeared. In these times we might well wonder if it was wisely done.

4

The Terrible Crone

4

There are many statues and paintings of the entity that Erich Neumann called the most grandiose form of the Terrible Mother: India's Kali Ma, the archetypal Crone. She represented "the hungry earth, which devours its own children and fattens on their corpses."[1] Here, his anthropomorphic statement demonstrates the male propensity to view feminine indifference as deadly, even when the femininity is only a figment of human imagination, and the indifference (of the inanimate) is only natural.

In her typical pose, Kali Ma squats on top of her consort Shiva, who lies dead under her feet. She rips open his belly, and drags his entrails into her mouth. Sometimes her vulva devours him sexually as well. She scowls fiercely. She sticks out her tongue. Her eyeballs bulge. Her hands—sometimes two, sometimes four—brandish symbols of the elements, which she controls. Around her neck she wears a necklace of human skulls, bearing the letters of the Sanskrit alphabet, the sacred language she invented at creation. Sometimes she has other grisly relics about her: lopped-off hands, feet, or penises. She is lean and wrinkled like a mummy. Her ribs protrude above a hollow, dessicated stomach. Despite the elaborate ornaments she wears, she is undeniably ugly. One can understand why the curators of the London museum labeled her image "Kali—Destroying Demon."[2]

However, there is a curious discrepancy between this laconic description and the scriptures of Kali's native land, which seem to regard her as the greatest of all deities.

She is the creatress of the universe, older than time, vaster than space. She is the cause and Mother of the world, the One Primordial Being.[3] She is "pure Being-Consciousness-Bliss," the power existing in the form of time and space, and everything they contain, the "radiant Illuminatrix in all beings."[4] She is the Great Cause, the Primordial Energy, the Great Effulgence, more subtle than the subtlest elements. The gods themselves said to her, "Thou art the Original of all manifestations; Thou art the birthplace of even Us; Thou knowest the whole world, yet none know

Thee. . . . Thou art the Beginning of all, Creatrix, Protectress, and Destructress."⁵

All gods were born of her body, and "at the time of dissolution" (doomsday) they would again disappear into her.⁶ She is the "material cause of all change, manifestation and destruction. . . . [T]he whole Universe rests upon Her, rises out of Her and melts away into Her. From Her are crystallized the original elements and qualities which construct the apparent worlds. She is both mother and grave."⁷ She is so vast that "the series of universes appear and disappear with the opening and shutting of her eyes."⁸ Obviously, there is more to this ugly Goddess than meets the Western eye; a description of her as only a "destroying demon" is woefully inadequate. A few decades ago, Vivekananda wrote of her: "One vision I see clear as life before me, that the ancient mother has awakened once more, sitting on her throne rejuvenated, more glorious than ever. Proclaim her to all the world with the voice of peace and benediction."⁹ How can such sincere reverence be applied to the monster we see in her portraits? Let us try to fathom this mystery.

To begin with, we must realize that the Destroyer named Kali was only one aspect of the many-named, multiform Goddess. Changeable as nature itself, she assumed all forms. She was both ugly and beautiful, Virgin and Crone, darkness and light, winter and summer, birth giver and death bringer. She was a truer image of the real world's variety and cyclic alternation than any of the images developed by patriarchy alone.

Kali's Oriental worshipers long ago understood that man's division of the natural world into "good" and "evil"—meaning what helps *man* survive, as opposed to what harms him—is an insignificant human wish, artificially imposed on a dispassionate universe. They recognized that the dynamic maintenance of the whole system requires constant simultaneous creation and destruction. Life forms cannot exist without destroying other life forms. And every form is temporary, running through its own cycle from burgeoning growth to decline, death, and decay.

They said also that the Goddess rules all cycles, therefore the second part of each cycle is no less sacred or important than the first. They tried to lay aside their human egoism by understanding that a human being exerts no more weight in the cosmic scheme of things than another animal, plant, or microbe. The yogis seriously tried to adopt a kind of humility that patriarchal thinkers gave only lip service. Thus they avoided the dualistic world view that forced Western worshipers of an "all-good" God to provide him with a devilish adversary, to account for the obvious presence of evil.

Even when certain kinds of destructiveness were (and are) referred to as "acts of God," Western thinkers paradoxically rejected the ancient view that a deity can shift unpredictably from benevolence to malice. Conversely, worshipers of Kali took their world view from nature, rather than from their own desires and preferences, and strove to realize a larger context for events. In this they were not unlike the ancient world's Gnostic, Stoic, Orphic, and Pythagorean sages, who counseled uncomplaining submission to Mother Fate—whether she was called Moera, Fortuna, Nemesis, Heimarmene, Dike, Persephone, or any other name. Kali's followers believed that true religion lay in reverent acceptance of the Goddess's decrees. They would have found unthinkable the medieval European concept of a world wholly focused on man's personal choice between good and evil, and of a universe viewed only as an enormous backdrop for the trivial drama of his personal salvation or damnation.

Though the Goddess's trinitarian character included many forms of the beautiful birth-giving Virgin and the protective Mother, yet it was the hideous death-dealing Crone who posed the true test of faith. As a nature worshiper learned to respect both the loveliness and the dangers of nature, so Kali's *shakta* (yogi) learned to adore both the pleasure and the fear inspired by women and by life. Of the adept, it was said: "His Goddess, his loving Mother in time, who gave him birth and loves him in the flesh, also destroys him in the flesh. His image of Her is incomplete if he does not know Her as his tearer and devourer."[10]

His god Shiva, called Lord of Yoga and Great God (Mahadeva), showed the way by offering up his own flesh and blood to the Goddess, who devoured and then resuscitated him. As in the prehistoric rites of cannibalistic communion, when women ate flesh and blood of the dead and caused them to be "born again" as new children, so the god had to be eaten by his Mother, who was also his spouse. Such was the original rationale of all communion rites, and the original means of resurrection for all sacrificed savior-gods.

The sages perceived the spirit of the Goddess as immanent in the bodies of all women. Therefore the true yogi "bows down at the feet of women, regarding them as his Guru." They said, "The Divine Mother first appears in and as Her worshiper's earthly mother, then as his wife; thirdly, as Kalika, She reveals Herself in old age, disease and death."[11] Among her many names, she had a name representing each of the deadly diseases, which is why uncomprehending Westerners sometimes described her as a Goddess of disease.[12] She encompassed all kinds of death: easy or hard, fast or slow, ranging from the death that comes too soon, before life's fulfillment, to the death that comes too late, after too much suffering.

In view of the Goddess's trinitarian character, Tantric Buddhism provided her with three corresponding classes of attendant spirits or priestesses: *yogini, matri, dakini* (Virgin, Mother, Crone). Like the nymphs that attended ancient Greek and Roman shrines of the Goddess, each class had both celestial and earthly incarnations.[13]

A *yogini* was like the "virgin bride of God" known as a *kadesha* in the ancient Near East. She could be a teacher, temple dancer (Hindu *devadasi*), sacred harlot, or exemplar of sexual rites where she might play the role of the Virgin Goddess as *alma mater* (soul mother), the god's or his worshiper's "dearly beloved."

Like the Graces or Horae of classical antiquity, celestial yoginis personified grace, beauty, artistic inspiration, mystical ecstasy, and love. Images of yoginis on Hindu temples closely resembled classical images of the naked, dancing Graces. Like mortal priestesses, yoginis were "virgin" not because they took no lovers, but because they took no husbands. Their children were considered god-begotten, and often reincarnations of the same god. Hence, they were not only virgin brides of the god, but also virgin mothers of the god. In the subsequent role of *matris* (mothers), they acquired additional prestige and religious authority.

Elder priestesses, celestial or terrestrial, were the *dakinis,* "sky-walkers."[14] Devoted to the Destroyer aspect of the Goddess's trinity, they prepared the fatally ill for death, counseled their families, governed funeral customs, and in spirit form (after their own rites of passage) led the way into the mysterious Land of the Intermediate State. "Gentle dakinis" or "fierce dakinis" in that mystic realm might be charged with the duty of rewarding the virtuous and punishing sinners.[15]

Often, in the process of caring for dying persons, a dakini was supposed to take the final breath of the deceased into herself with the "kiss of peace," signifying the Goddess's acceptance of the wandering soul. There were similar female psychopomps in non-Christian Western tradition, such as the Slavic *vilas,* Teutonic *valkyries,* or Celtic Morrigan (banshee). It was said of them also that they could bring the dead soul to a rebirth by sucking it into themselves with the final kiss, and that death in their arms could be sweet and painless, even ecstatic.

The dakini's title of skywalker identified her as a spirit of the air. The nearest Western approximation was *sylph,* an elemental spirit of the air. Like all other words for a pagan death priestess, this too became a synonym for a witch. French laws of the early ninth century forbade "sylphs" to manifest themselves, on pain of heavy penalties.[16] Such "sylphs" were probably real women, but through their connection with the heavens and the afterlife, they were believed capable of flying through the air—on broomsticks, angel wings, winged animals, or as shapeshifters in their own alternate forms of birds, bats, and butterflies (*psyches,* meaning both "butterfy" and "soul").

In all cultures, flying was the archetypal model of the soul's journey to heaven. Many traditions suggested that it could be done several times before a final death, especially with the help of a female adept, like the pre-Islamic Arabian priestess known as a *fravashi* or "Spirit of the Way," who was virtually indistinguishable from a Tantric temple maiden, or one of the "fairy ladies" of European legend. Eurasian shamans couldn't practice until they completed an initiatory death and resurrection, with a soul journey to heaven. In this, a shaman required the help of a female guardian angel, a celestial wife or mistress, or the earthly embodiment of such a being, who was often supposed to be able to change her shape to that of a bird.[17] As medieval "witches," the same skywalkers, sylphs, fairies, or guardian angels were thought able to transform themselves into owls, crows, swans, and other aerial creatures. Flying ointments and broomstick flights owed much to these traditions.

Careful comparison of the Oriental dakini with the Occidental crone priestess can only establish their common origin. Like the vast family of Indo-European languages, Indo-European religions also reveal their mutual ancestress. As Kali and Eve shared the same title, "Mother of All Living," so sacred women both East and West shared the same perceptions of the meaning of life and death. "As among the gods, so among the mortals was death everywhere woman's business. . . . Women cradle the infant and the corpse, each to its particular new life."[18]

It was commonly claimed that European witches held nocturnal ceremonies in graveyards. So did the dakinis. Devotees of Kali the Destroyer gathered by night in the gruesome atmosphere of cremation grounds to familiarize themselves with the sights and smells of death, to overcome their fear.[19] It may be that the witches of the West remembered a similar tradition. The *Kalevala* even gave the name of Kalma (Kali Ma) to the Goddess who reigned over graves, and repeated the image of Black Kali as Mother of Diseases, in its black-featured mother of such spirits as Pleurisy, Colic, Gout, Phthisis, Ulcers, Scabies, Canker, and Plague.[20]

Gypsies worshiped the same Mother of Diseases as their Goddess Sara-Kali (Queen Kali), under her Crone title of Bibi, "the Aunt," who dressed in red like the blood-clothed Kali of the Hindu doomsday.[21] The gypsies said she "has the power to cause all kinds of disease, especially at the beginning of a new month when there is a full moon."[22] For hundreds of years, beginning about the ninth century, gypsies migrated westward to Europe from their original home in Hindustan, where Kali was regarded as their supreme deity. Naturally, they brought their Goddess with them.

But Kali's appearances in the West were older than gypsy migrations. She had been carried westward in the prehistoric period by some of the earliest Indo-European tribes, who later became her "Aryan" peoples: Celts, Teutons, Goths, Gaels, Saxons, Franks, Danes, and so on. Their common myths of the Goddess-ruled Western paradise, far over the rim of the horizon, indicate that their migrations might have originally followed the westward movements of sun, moon, and stars to find the cosmic Womb of Rebirth where all these celestial spirits went at their setting.

As far from India as prehistoric migrants could travel, namely in northern Britain, we find Kali-the-Crone still under what is almost her original name: Caillech, meaning the Old Woman, Hag, Crone, or Veiled One.[23] Scottish, Irish, and Welsh legends said the Caillech was, like Kali, a black-faced Goddess who created the world and gave birth to its races of people. She had many husbands. They died one after another, like Kali's constantly slain and resurrected consorts.

When the Caillech was forming the earth, she dropped huge stones out of her apron to create mountain ranges. The Welsh sometimes called her the Hag of the Dribble, because the mountains "dribbled" from her garment. The same Hag was identified as a Death Goddess, flapping her raven wing against the window of each person doomed to die, calling to the soul in a voice like that of the banshee or Morrigan.[24]

The Morrigan, or Morgan, was a typical Celtic female trinity, especially associated with the Western Isles of the Dead, or Fortunate Isles, or Avalon the "Apple-land," where she gave the blessed dead her magic apples of immortality from the Tree of Life.[25] In common with Eve's tree in Eden, this recalls the Goddess's magic Rose-Apple Tree on Jambu Island, the Hindu Western paradise.[26] Many other versions of the pagan fairyland were based on the same image. Ancient people often believed their honored dead became stars (or luminous angels) in heaven, immortal because the Mother gave them daily rebirth as they passed from her Western gate under the earth to the East. This gate of the dead was located, naturally, in the West. Even the Eskimos spoke of a Western land of the dead known as the Old Woman's Dwelling.[27] We still say that to die is to "go West."

The Western Caillech was also a Kali-like Mother of Diseases. An Irish idol of her is extant, known as the Goddess of Smallpox, to which afflicted persons used to sacrifice sheep.[28] Scottish legend said of the Caillech that she sometimes had one eye in the middle of her forehead, like statues of Kali with her central "third eye" of mystical insight; and that she gave birth to monstrous giants with several heads and arms apiece: obvious recollections of typically Hindu deities.[29]

It seems the westward-moving prehistoric Aryans forgot the esoteric meanings of their ancestral deities' multiple heads and arms, and became convinced that these old idols were ugly. The Scandinavian myth of the many-armed god Starkad shows a

Hindu-style statue subjected to cosmetic amputations. The myth said the god Thor tore off all but two of Starkad's arms, to make him handsomer, though his body bore the scars of his supernumerary limbs ever afterward. Starkad was one of the older gods called *risi*, a cognate of Sanskrit *rishi*, a sage.[30]

Among other indications of Kali in the West was the mysterious Irish deity known as Kele-De, the Goddess Kele, or sometimes Kale. Her devotees were known as *kelles*, a word perhaps once applied to promiscuous priestesses belonging to a sacred clan, origin of the name Kelly. Irish writings described the holy harlot Mary Magdalene as a *kelle*.[31] Kele-De has been translated several ways, in addition to its basic meaning, the Goddess Kele. Some monkish writers claimed it meant "spouse of God," or "companion of God," or even "servant of God." Toward the end of the seventh century A.D., the term was used for certain contemplative sects of hermits or anchorites, not too different from the contemplative yogis. Other versions of their title were Ceile-De or Culdee. It seems certain that these Culdees were religious sectaries of some kind, but medieval Christian writers knew little about them. Their history is shrouded in silence.[32]

There were other indications of a Kali cult in the British Isles. One of Kali's many names as a fertile Earth Mother was Tara: the same name given the Earth Mother's shrine in pagan Ireland. One of Tara's early god-kings, Eremon, may have been the Hindu god Aryaman, ancestor of "Aryans." Another Irish god, the Horned One, Cernunnos, was represented in the cross-legged lotus position of a yogi—the same position that churchmen later called a symptom of heresy.[33]

Indian yogis believed their discipline could develop the magic quality of *siddhi*, control of elemental forces. A master who reached such a high level as, for instance, Siddhartha Buddha (the Buddha rich in *siddhi*), could walk on water, heal the sick, exorcise demons, turn base metal into gold, and similar miracles. Scandinavian Aryans said their ancient race of *risis* (*rishis*, sages) developed a magic power called *seidr*, which originally belonged to women, and could be learned only from the Great Goddess, Freya.[34] That this was *siddhi* might be deduced from other cognates also: Moorish *sidi* (sage or hero) became the Spanish title of El Cid; *sihr* was a Sufi word for "sage's power"; the Lapps called spirit-power *seidi;* the

Celts spoke of fairy lore as the *sidh,* and the underground fairyland with its Queen's castle, Caer Sidi. This strange revolving structure was the hub of the (karmic) wheel of the world.[35]

In pre-Christian Rome, the Goddess Juno bore exactly the same title as Kali-Durga: Juno the Preserver, Queen of the Mothers.[36] She, too, was a trinity of Virgin, Mother, and Crone, in her early Sabine incarnation as the Capitoline Triad, united under the name of Uni, Mother of the Uni-verse. Though her Virgin form was later replaced by the young male god Jove, she was originally an all-female trinity: Juventas the maiden, Juno the Mother, and Minerva the wise Crone.

The famous three colors of the female trinity were the same in northwestern Europe and southeastern Asia: white, red, and black. These colors were known in India as her *gunas* or "strands." As the sacred colors of Kali-Maya, the Creatress, or "the divine female Prakriti," they represented (1) radiant, pure tranquility; (2) blazing energy and passion; and (3) weight and darkness, the silent night of the tomb. All creation was woven of the Virgin's white *(sattva),* the Mother's red *(rajas),* and the Crone's black *(tamas).* [37]

These colors were seen by a hero in the underworld as the web of time, nights and days (black and white) woven together with the blood-red thread of life.[38] In another interpretation, the three colors stood for (1) presentation of consciousness; (2) action; and (3) veiling of consciousness—in other words, birth, life, death.[39]

Western thinkers too were familiar with these tricolored strands of fate, always woven by the Triple Goddess. Theocritus, Ovid, and Horace said the threads of life were colored white, red, and black.[40] Sumerian temples were faced with clay-cone mosaics in the same three colors.[41] The white, red, and black decorated horned, sacred vessels in prehistoric Chalcolithic cultures of the Balkan Peninsula.[42]

The white, red, and black appeared everywhere in religious myths and fairy tales of Celtic origin. They were the colors of the Hounds of Annwn, the underworld dogs of death. They were the colors of the female attendants (priestesses) in the castle of the Holy Grail, which began as the mystic castle of Peredur's secret initiation in pagan Welsh tradition. Peredur worshiped a "divine maiden" with a snow-white complexion, blood-red cheeks, and jet-black hair. His love was so great that at the sight of her colors alone—crow's feathers and blood drops in the snow—he fell into a curiously yogic trance of contemplation.[43] The same mysterious beauty became Snow White in a later fairy tale, sometimes with a sister named Rose Red. These might be identified with Druidic sacred queens, Eithne the Fair and Fedelim the Rosy.[44]

The wicked stepmother of such popular fairy tales probably represented the black Crone; she was often described as "dark." The fear she inspired would have suggested the storytellers' conversion of her from a true mother to a stepmother, so she would be more believable in the role of Destroyer, after her close symbolic connection with the destroying motherhood of Nature was obscured or forgotten.

Christians generally displaced the fear inspired by the Goddess onto their favorite scapegoat, the devil—and of course, on his alleged servants, the witches. Accordingly, Dante gave his literary Lucifer three faces, after the manner of Hecate, Queen of Witches: one face white, the second red, the third black. Yet in Dante's time it was a church custom to lay three veils on the altar, to remove one at each nocturn of Christmas matins; the colors of the veils were white, red, and black.[45]

This was only one of many survivals within Christianity of the rituals and symbols of the pagan Goddess, other than the figure of Mary, a combination of Virgin and Mother. Before the sixteenth century, the Crone in her ugliness was built into the very fabric of Irish churches. Naked sheila-na-gig figures "protected" the doors and windows of such churches, just as naked figures of Kali squatted at the doors of Hindu temples, where worshipers passing through the portal would reverently touch their carved genitalia (the Gate of Life).[46]

The Irish sheila-na-gig might have represented the Caillech. She certainly resembled Kali. Lean and skeletal, like a mummy, with protruding rib cage, such a figure typically squatted with widely separated knees, displaying her holy yoni (vulva) in the form of a *vesica piscis* (vertical double-pointed oval): the same sign that often appeared in Kali's geometrical *yantras* (meditation diagrams).

During the nineteenth century, the blatant obscenity of the sheila-na-gig figures was called to the attention of church authorities, who then had many of them defaced, or hacked out of the stonework and destroyed. Some were found later, buried near the churches they formerly decorated.[47] Nonetheless, Irish peasants never ceased to believe that doorways should be protected with a female genital symbol, such as a horseshoe. This shape too was sacred to Kali, representing her *Om* or Word (Logos) of Creation. Her spouse Shiva performed his sexual dance within a horseshoe of fire, representing the cosmic yoni. The symbol passed into the Greek alphabet as the Crone's letter, the horseshoe-shaped omega, which means literally "great Om."

When Goddess-worshiping ceremonies persisted among medieval Europeans, churches often tolerated or even supported them, after inventing a new legend to provide a Christianized rationale. Many pagan customs survived as spring processionals, Maypole dances, solstitial bonfires, harvest homes, well dressings, carnival games, and other remnants of the ancient sacred drama.

One of the most persistent of these remnants in England was the annual ride of Lady Godiva, whose name descended from Indo-European *devi* or *diva,* meaning "Goddess." She was also called Goda or Gerd, the Gothic Freya. Her divine spouse was Godan (Wotan).[48] At Southam she appeared as twins, the White Goddess and the Black Goddess, the latter virtually identical with Kali.[49] The nursery rhyme described her as "the fine lady on a white horse," but some versions made it "the old woman on a white horse."[50]

Godiva was mortalized by a Christian revision, invented to explain her naked ride through Coventry as a penance imposed on her by a human husband. However, this was recognized as "a mere fable."[51] As a standard feature of agricultural paganism, the ride on May Eve of the Naked Goddess was thought necessary to bless the fields. It continued even though clergymen ordered the people to stay indoors and refrain from watching it. Hence the legendary lack of spectators for Godiva's ride, except for "Peeping Tom." As the May-maiden symbolizing fertility, the Crone's other face, she appeared in European countries under such names as May, Maj, Maga, Maia, or Maya, all variants of the Hindu Maya, virgin mother of the savior Buddha.

Like the Christian savior, the Buddhist savior took on the character of a conqueror of death, often mythologized as a divine son's rejection or destruction of his mother. The ascetic Buddhist tradition claimed that Buddha's virgin mother Maya "died of joy" shortly after his birth, even though she lived on forever as "the soul manifested in matter" for all the world.[52]

Wherever the savior's resurrection was adapted from older Goddess-oriented versions of the death-and-rebirth theme, his tomb and womb were the same; that is, his Bride, Mother, and Destroyer were all the same Goddess. Even Jesus, like most other savior-gods of his time, was laid in a virgin tomb, "wherein was never man yet laid" (John 19:41). Many other gods had a similar rebirth from the tomb-womb, announced by women only, as in the Bible story of Mary Magdalene and the women (or priestesses) who accompanied her (Luke 24:10–11).

The Gospels showed Jesus rejecting his mother on several occasions, saying he had nothing to do with her (John 2:4), or he recognized no relation with her (Mark 3:33). This may have been an allegorical rejection of death, for Mary or Mara was an ancient name of Mother Death in most Eastern lands. The Buddhist savior rejected her in the form of a love-and-death spirit, Kama-Mara, sometimes called a "demon" who tempted him. The demon who tempted Jesus was identified with Satan rather than with Mara; yet her death curse appears in the Gospels as Maranatha (Mary-Anath) according to 1 Corinthians 16:22.

The whole premise of Christianity was, like ascetic Buddhism, that to achieve a rejection of death, man must reject the Mother manifested in all women, including his own mother. Rosemary Radford Ruether says, "Male eschatology is built on negation of the mother. . . . The escape from sex and birth is ultimately an attempt to escape from death for which women as Eve and mother are made responsible. Male eschatology combines male womb envy with womb negation."[53] The life given by Mother was always cyclic, never eternal. For some men, it was never enough. They wanted a life everlasting. Therefore, some Buddhists rejected Kali, just as Christians rejected Mara-Anatha, or Morgan, or Hel, or Cerridwen, or the Caillech, or any of dozens of other manifestations of the Crone.

Kali-the-Crone was black because she represented the great darkness at both the beginning and the end of life's "daytime" or conscious cycle. She was also the infinite void at both the beginning and the end of the universe. She was naked (*digambara*), "clothed in space alone."[54] At the end of time, she would swallow up all existence. All created things, including gods, would disappear again into her darkness as "colors all disappear in black."[55] In a sense, this vision of Kali was not unlike modern scientific scenarios for the creation of suns and solar systems out of gradually coalescing dark clouds of particles and gas. Kali's method of creating the universe out of the darkness of herself was often described as a curdling or clotting process, similar to the clotting of retained menstrual blood that the ancients believed responsible for forming the child in the womb. Like blood solidifying, Kali's primal liquidlike "chaos" held all the elements in an unformed flux or state of potentiality, then created solid matter out of itself.

A similar creation myth was found in the Orphic Mysteries. The great primeval power was Mother Night (Nyx), dreaded even by the father of gods. Like Kali, she too was both Creator and Destroyer. In the beginning she arose from chaos and gave birth to the light.[56] She took the form of a great black-winged spirit hovering over a sea of darkness: the "face of the Deep," as biblical writers would have it (Gen. 1:2), though they forgot the original sex of the creating spirit.[57]

The biblical version adapted the basic creation myth to the limitations of a male god, who couldn't give birth; therefore he somehow produced the first light just by pronouncing its name. Bible writers made the mistake, however, of having their god bring this light into being several days before he made its source, the sun. This is a common mistake of primitive people, who often assume that daylight and sunlight are not the same thing.

Mother Night or Nyx also gave birth to Love, Fate, Sleep, Dreams, Nemesis, Old Age, and Death—and of course, the nixies, which were late "fairy tale" versions of her attendants. The Egyptians had their own vision of her, known as Nu, Nut, Nuit, or Neith, Goddess of Black Night, out of whose watery womb the sun arose for the first time at creation, and to which all things must return. She existed before earth and heaven were differentiated from one another, and before there were any gods. She was of fathomless depth and boundless extent.[58] Scandinavian myths had the same Mother Night, who gave birth to the three Fates (Norns), her own trinitarian nature manifested as rulers of the past, present, and future.[59]

Certain early Christian Gnostic sectaries wrote of a similar primeval female source, out of which came the original seven Powers, Roots, or Aeons at the beginning of time. Simon Magus said God the Father came out of her too, but he was not called Father until she had so named him.[60]

The combination of Kali and Shiva in their eternal union made an androgyne, Ardhanarisvara, whom the Persians adopted as a half-masculine Crone figure named Zurvan, "Infinite Time." From her womb came both God and the devil as twin brothers, Ahura Mazda and Ahriman—the latter, another transformation of the Hindu god Aryaman. Like Cain and Abel, one of these gods became good and rose to heaven because he offered the right sacrifices; the other became evil and was cast down to the underworld because he offered the wrong ones.[61] He became the Great Serpent who lived in the bowels of the earth and knew the secrets of the primal Goddess because he lived near the roots of her power.

Another definition of Zurvan was "decrepitude," that is, old age, like the Caillech, or the Teutonic Elli. Her Kali-like character made her a rather awesome image of decrepitude, hinting at the fear with which men sometimes regarded old women. Zurvan was said to be totally incomprehensible to limited human knowledge. She was unapproachable. She was a being to whom a man dared not speak.[62] In this context we might remember Durga the Inaccessible, also called Queen of the Mothers.

The Crone's bearing of both God and devil was an expression of the basically Tantric and Gnostic idea that good and evil were identical in origin, therefore all spirit was of the same nature. If good and evil were twins, all human souls with their mixtures of good and evil were just offshoots of the same primal Oversoul that gave birth to both, and to whom both would return to be remixed for another cycle. This concept of the identity of all spirit as discrete portions of the same World Soul was anathema to orthodox Christianity. Naturally, it would make absurdities of Christian notions of postmortem reward and punishment. The salvation marketed by the church would become irrelevant. Though the idea did occur in early Gnostic Christianity, it was soon declared heretical. After all, to follow the idea to its logical conclusion, the church would have had to eliminate those very services for which it received most of its income.

The Black Goddess, who took all soul-stuff back into herself, was fundamental not only in Tantric and Gnostic belief, but also in paganism generally, throughout pre-Christian Europe. In Scandinavia, one of her primary manifestations was the underground Goddess Hel, Queen of the Ghostworld or Queen of the Shades. Though her subterranean realm gave the English language its *hell,* Hel's country was not a place of punishment. It was only the dark womb, symbolized by the cave, cauldron, pit, well, or mountain interior, to which the dead returned, and from which they could be regenerated. Old Norse *hellir* meant "a cave," like similar caves in Mediterranean lands sacred to the underground Crone. Iceland's home of the dead lay beneath Hel's western mountain, Helgafell.[63]

Even in the Middle Ages, under Teutonic names like Frau Holde or Dame Holle, Hel remained the guardian of pagan souls. She took care of all children who died unbaptized.[64] Some said all children in the process of birth came forth from "Dame Holle's Pond," the universal womb.[65] When she took heroes into her womb of death, they were known as Helleder, "those who belong to Hel."[66] Celtiberian medals showed the Lord of Death as Helman, "the spouse of Hel."[67] Sometimes, like the underground god Hades, he wore the conical cap of darkness, *Helkappe,* a *hel*met that could render its wearer invisible, like a ghost. While wearing it, he could come and go at will between the earthly world and the subterranean world of the dead.[68]

Some myths said men who died in battle were exempt from the rule of Hel. She took the souls of people who died of illness, accident, or old age.[69] Battle-slain heroes belonged to Father Odin, not to the matriarchal Goddess Hel. Heroes would go to Odin's palace at Asgard, and enjoy daily combat, followed by drinking and feasting. Their wounds would heal overnight, so they could begin all over again the next day.

Obviously, this was a religion of war, similar to the Islamic notion of the heroes' heaven, which promised soldierly defenders of the faith an eternal bliss among supersexy divine houris. Nevertheless, Scandinavian heroes were picked up from the battlefield by some direct descendants of Kali's dakinis, the celestial death priestesses known as Valkyries.

Without these psychopomps to bear their souls aloft, heroes would never get to Asgard. As female spirits pressed into the service of a patriarchal, militaristic religion, the Valkyries survived in popular belief at least to the eleventh century, when King Canute's laws spoke of certain witches called *walcyries* or "Choosers of the Slain."[70] Valkyries were also shapeshifters, able to take animal forms such as mares, swans, or hawks. Their most common bird form was that of the carrion crow, sacred to the Black Crone. The Valkyrie Brunnhilde (Burning Hel) often took the shape and name of Krake, "Crow."[71]

Another name for Hel was Skadi, the Black One, literally "a shade or shadow" (Gothic *skadus,* Old English *sceadu*). Celts called her Scatha or Scath. Their underworld was "the Land of Scath."[72] All Scandinavia was originally sacred to her, when it was Scadinauja, "the Land of Skadi."[73] She was the all-devouring shadow into which the gods would pass at doomsday, the time of their ultimate dissolution. This occurrence was mythologized as Götterdämmerung, usually translated "the Twilight of the gods"; but its literal meaning is "Going-Into-the-Shadow of the gods."[74]

Because of her intrinsically fearsome character and her absolute power over even the most heroic and grandiose male gods, the Crone was readily diabolized by male-centered religions. Naturally, she was the ultimate castrator, bringing impotence as the inevitable concomitant of sickness, old age, and death. This was emphasized in myths and symbolism that made her the collector of severed penises, or the receiver of the sacrificed savior's genitals, as in the Mysteries of Cybele and Attis, Venus and Adonis, Anath and Baal, and so on. The Norse Goddess collected penises under her Crone name of Mörnir, Troll-Woman. She took the amputated penis of the sacrificial horse, which embodied the spirit of Odin himself.[75] Men tended to forget that the original crude castration ceremonies were instituted by their own sex, when male ancestors tried to appropriate the biological magic of the female.

Castration fears were evident in the most obsessive fantasies of medieval churchmen, who wrote of witches' theft of men's penises as if they had no doubt of its occurrence. Official literature of the Inquisition said it "has been seen by many and is a matter of common report" that witches sometimes collected as many as twenty or thirty male organs together, and kept them in a box or a bird's nest.[76] The conviction peculiar to males that sex organs have an uncontrollable, independent life of their own, is expressed in the churchmen's belief that the stolen penises moved about and ate food in their captivity, like animals.

From Terrible Crone to castrating witch was not a large step, especially since patriarchal thinkers showed themselves willing to stoop to any vilification of female powers. Even the Christian vision of hell, the most sadistic fantasy in man's history, was named for, and blamed on, several versions of the ancient Mother. Even the version that became the virtual Goddess of the Western world, under the name of Mary, had other, diabolized offshoots from her ancient Near Eastern prototype, the Goddess Mari, or Marah, or Mara-Anatha.

Nightmares were attributed to the female death spirit descended from Kali-Mara, later the Buddhist love-and-death demon Kama-Mara.[77] An old name for a clan matriarch, *mara* or *mair*, meaning an old woman—origin of the French *maire*, English *mayor*—also entered modern European languages as a name of horror, the Night-Mare. In Swedish, she was *Mara*; in German, *Nachtmar*.[78] An alternate name for the Night-Mare was the Druidess, or Franconian *die Drud*, which became the English *Trot*, a colloquialism for an old woman.[79]

The Night-Mare could take literal equine form as a black mare, a mare-headed demon, or a shapeshifting horse-Valkyrie. In Scandinavian mythology the horse was a death symbol. Norse skalds said a man rides to the land of death on a horse or a mare.[80] In Greece, black mare-headed Demeter dwelt underground in sacred caves and became a Destroyer under her alternate names of Persephone, Demeter Chthonia (Subterranean Demeter), or Erinys (Avenger). The Orphic manual of the Mysteries, *The Descent Into Hades*, proclaimed her the Death Mother who would have mercy on the initiate who repeated her holy formulas, such as "I have sunk beneath the bosom of Persephone, Queen of the Underworld."[81]

Like the Celtic Death Mother Cerridwen, Demeter was "the source of life, and the receptacle of the dead."[82] One of her Cretan names was Melanippe, "Black Mare." Another of her Cretan names, Rhea, gave rise to the Celtic Goddess Rhiannon, the same Earth Mother who ate her own children. Often her Night-Mare character was a personification of conscience, for the Goddess sent ominous dreams to warn or to torment those who broke her laws.

The ancients considered all dreams in some sense prophetic. They took dream images seriously, as communications from a divine source. When Demeter assumed the character of the Night-Mare and sent frightening dreams, men assumed she was mobilizing her avenging demons against them. Thus the divine Ancestress who knew all secrets, from whom nothing could be hidden, became a figure of fear.

Mara, Mari, or Ishtar-Mari was also associated with the oceans (*maria*), thus likened to the devouring Deep which was also the cosmic womb. Marah, "Sea," was a title taken by biblical Naomi when she entered her Crone phase. People who practiced ship burial were particularly respectful of the pelagian Mara. To the Danes, Marae or Marraminde meant a "wisewoman of the sea." Norwegians called her Maerin, or Mare-mynd. Germans called her the Mereminne. Englishmen called her the mermaid.[83] As fish-tailed Aphrodite Marina, she gradually merged with the Virgin Mary, whose blue robe and foam-white pearl necklace were recognized by the pagans as symbolic of the maternal sea. One of her numerous Greek trinitarian forms had the related name of Moera, whose Virgin-Mother-Crone personae were Clotho the Spinner, Lachesis the Measurer, and Atropos the Cutter (of the thread of life).

There was an old temple of this Goddess at Inis Maree (Mari's Isle) in Scotland, which was destroyed early in the Christian era. Still, people continued to sacrifice bulls on the same site each year on the Goddess's holy day in August, all the way up to the seventeenth century. To account for this curious custom, the church eventually adopted the Goddess under the name of Saint Mourie, though none could explain why a saint should be worshiped with offerings at a ruined pagan temple.[84]

Male-dominant societies often tried to simplify the complex Goddess by dissecting a saint or madonna stereotype out of her multifaceted character. The only kind of Goddess men desired was the infant's ideal: a beautiful, complaisant, ever-loving, ever-attentive young Mother in her most devotedly nurturant phase. Her other aspects were labeled evil, especially the sex-goddess and Crone phases. As for a baby or child phase: this was recognized only in male divinities. The female was always full grown, responsible, and capable of taking care of her dependent boy. Modern psychology might find much food for thought in this ubiquitous imagery. Men's gods could appear as infants and also as white-bearded patriarchs, implying a more or less normal lifespan for the deities man made in his own image. However, if the Goddess was permitted in any form, she was assumed to be one-dimensional, frozen in one facet of her being. Women were expected to emulate her, against all reason.

Psychology has only recently recognized the persistence of infantile longings in men's attitudes toward women, even though clues were never lacking: for instance, the adult male's obsession with breasts. Another clue is the typically patriarchal tendency to reject aging women, whose "old mother" image tends to emphasize the son's chronological maturity. When a man sees that the same body that produced him, nourished him, and carried him through his most dependent, formative years, must itself succumb to time's theft of its strength, he may become unconsciously frightened. In Kali's graveyard ceremonies, her conspicuously withered body was designed to force the worshiper to confront the realities of decline and decay; to seize the nettle, as it were; to learn to alleviate fear by facing the object of fear head-on.

Interestingly, Crone and sex-goddess phases often overlapped, or even coalesced, in this Oriental imagery. No matter how hideous her appearance, Kali's sexuality was never understated. Indeed, her devouring sexuality was seen as one of her most fearsome aspects. It was supposed infinitely more powerful than that of her consort, perhaps even the cause of his death.

The asceticism of religious hermits, East or West, might be partly attributable to male fear of such voracious female sexuality. However titillating men might find their own fantasy images of the sexually insatiable female, they may be seen to retreat in frantic haste from anything resembling its reality. The official literature of the medieval Inquisition stated that all witchcraft could be attributed to carnal lust "which is in women insatiable."[85]

Male-centered religions' denial of death was inevitably confused with denial of sex, for the very reason that man's "little death" in sexual intercourse was viewed as a foretaste of the ultimate death represented by the fearsome Goddess. To the extent, however slight, that the elder woman might resemble that fearsome image, she was hastily rejected as a possible sexual partner.

This patriarchal ploy accomplished several purposes at once. For one thing, it gave husbands a good excuse to ignore the sexual appetite of aging wives, when the husbands themselves experienced declining sexual capacity in their middle age. It has been established that women commonly retain the capacity for sexual pleasure to a later age than men, even though men equally commonly blame their sexual failures on their wives.[86] Since patriarchal societies typically restricted their definition of male sexual function to intercourse with penetration and orgasm, their men were forced to save face somehow when they became less capable of this particular activity. It was made easy for a husband to divert guilt feelings from his own physiology to his wife's wrinkled face or sagging body, compelling her to accept additional shame for growing old: if she suffered sexual frustration, it was her fault, not his.

Another cherished tenet of patriarchal religion was that the proper purpose of sexual activity is to provide women with babies, not pleasure. Even in the 1970s, the official position of the Catholic church was that only the "finality" of procreation can justify marital sex, which is otherwise devoid of "moral goodness."[87] Obviously, by such reasoning a postmenopausal woman able to enjoy sex would be a moral evil. Yet it has been persuasively suggested that postmenopausal women often enjoy sex more, for the very reason that their fear of unwanted pregnancy has been relieved. From the patriarchal viewpoint, such pleasure is illicit and should be denied them.

Patriarchal rules also show that men didn't want to see any diminution in women's nurturing instinct, even at that stage of life when such diminution would normally take place. One of the least understood or least tolerated manifestations of the older woman's personality is her withdrawal from the abundantly other-directed behavior patterns of her mothering period, into a more self-directed mode of life, the change usually more or less coincident with menopause.

At this important turning point, many women openly express their intention to begin living for themselves, after years of self-abnegating devotion to husbands and/or children. Such women may return to school, take new jobs or hobbies, develop new kinds of friendships, cease to care whether men find them attractive or not. A husband may feel uneasy about his aging wife's newfound independence, which he perceives (perhaps correctly) as a measure of indifference to his personal well-being. Grown children want their own independence. Yet, at the same time, they may feel psychically abandoned by the mother who no longer centers her life around them, but instead pursues her own interests, which allow her little time for thinking of her offspring any more.

We hear much about women's nest-building instincts, which, after all, form the economic foundation of our consumer society; but we hear little of any nest-destroying behavior, which may be equally instinctive, as represented by several versions of the Crone. An older woman may experience strong urges to weed out her possessions, to simplify her life by purging it of excessive impedimenta, to move to smaller quarters and keep them neater, to restrict her social contacts to a few good friends instead of a wide circle of acquaintances. She may give things away, neglect her house, stop buying clothes. If she is still acquisitive, it may be only in respect to a personal enthusiasm, such as a collection, unrelated to the interests of other family members.

The mind of a postmenopausal woman is virtually uncharted territory, for men have shown little inclination to explore it. Doctors and psychiatrists glibly ascribe any or all of her difficulties to "menopausal depression," or a similar diagnostic catchall. However, it may be that her real needs and urges simply are not understood, so the experts have no jargon to describe them, just as our society has no symbol to represent them.

Earlier societies apparently understood more about the nest-destroying stage. Kali's adepts of both sexes were expected to retire from participation in the life of clan and community, for one or more retreat periods, after they had had their marriages and raised their children. Some would leave their families and possessions behind for good, simplifying existence down to the bare necessities. Alone in the forest, or in anchorite communities, they would turn their attention toward the oncoming end of life. Through introspection, they would seek revelation of the world's ultimate meaning, or lack of meaning. This final stage of life's activity became the Buddhist *moksha* or "liberation," also called "the art of dying." Its chief purpose was to achieve a glimpse of the Goddess without her veil, however terrifying she may appear.

Another function of the retreat was to accustom one's family to the idea of departure, so the elder's actual death would not elicit the angry sense of having been abandoned, which is an unspoken, but nevertheless common reaction, of survivors in our culture.

Such cyclic retreat from life's activity, a reversal corresponding to the burgeoning awareness and involvement of life's youthful stage, probably formed the foundation of ascetic ideals generally, which patriarchal cults eventually turned to their own advantage. In the latter, men renounced women for the sake of their own immortal souls, equating sex with death, as usual. However, these customs, like many others, seem to have been established by women in the first place. Pre-Christian religions often had communities of female anchorites, regarded as holy women, whose shrines were later transformed into Christian convents.

Based as it is on feminine support, our society dislikes the idea that women can lose interest in their families, sometimes with startling suddenness, and simply walk away to a new lifestyle. Yet it was observed early in the Christian era that the new faith was able to win many of the Roman women because they "fell in love with the doctrine of purity and separated from their husbands."[88]

Though animal behavior obviously is not supported by any such intellectual doctrines, most species in nature display similar tendencies. Once the male has served his reproductive purpose, the female usually rejects him. Once her young have grown old enough to live on their own, she casts them also out of the nest and destroys it.

Although man has often metaphorically regarded woman as a force of nature, he would rather not recognize any of her potential for rejection, preferring to see both Mother Nature and her human daughter as forever benevolent toward him. Even as metaphor, however, this is as unrealistic as the denial of death. Woman can't always be expected to lavish all her care upon man. Certainly Nature can't. It has been sagely remarked that Mother Nature "neither weeps nor rejoices. She produces man without purpose and obliterates him without regret."[89] Therefore, in the ancient religions based on appreciation of the cyclic Goddess, a place was made for the inevitable abandonment of the individual by the universal Mother's life-supporting power. Man didn't make his "meaning" contingent on perpetual continuation of what was clearly designed to be only temporary: that is, himself.

This concept may be difficult for Westerners to grasp. We are used to talking of the "meaning" of life, without ever stating what, in our view, life actually does mean. The idea that life might mean nothing at all, but simply *be,* is regarded as an Oriental subtlety that must be reinterpreted for the naive Western mind, which can't bear such a peek into the void. We prefer to think our undefined "meaning" has something to do with perpetuity of life after death, though in what form and by what mechanism we have not the least notion, and would rather not try to say.

What was usually called the search for meaning was typical of patriarchal philosophy, and undoubtedly related to the new perception of the supreme deity as a father figure. Fathers, not mothers, demanded that children justify their existence. Mothers accepted and loved their children unconditionally, just because they were there. The idea that one must have a reason for being was an idea developed by the divine father's sons, not by the divine mother's daughters.

Just as one needed a reason for living, under patriarchal systems, so also one needed a reason for dying. Always acceptable was a heroic death in battle, for a cause determined by one's chieftains, and upon their orders as surrogate fathers. Martyrdom was acceptable too, even self-sought martyrdom, which was supposed somehow to augment the Father's glory. Yet suicide was unacceptable, because it was an independent decision, not obedient to the Father's will. The medieval inquisition made suicide a heretical crime, conveniently punishable by ecclesiastical confiscation of the offender's worldly goods. Thus his guiltless heirs paid the penalty of his sin, and the church waxed fatter on their involuntary contributions.

Forms of the church's punitive laws against suicide survived into modern times, when they were found equally convenient for state and federal governments, insurance companies, and the courts. Suicide is still illegal in our culture, even for those who are terminally ill, in great pain, and desirous of death. To keep such individuals alive is so cruel that even our pet animals, through euthanasia, are generally spared this peculiarly human torment.

When the simple concept of an implacable female Fate or cyclically destructive Crone Mother was lost, Western attitudes toward death and dying took on oddly illogical shapes. For instance, there was the doctrine of resurrection of the flesh, which led to an entire industry of corpse preservation, as elaborate as mummification in ancient Egypt. There was also the idea promulgated by the early church that no matter how many crimes a man committed in life, deathbed rituals of Christian baptism and absolution could wipe out all his guilt and guarantee him a privileged place in heaven.

The emperor Constantine I was a happy beneficiary of this deathbed magic, after an unrepentant lifetime of treachery, warfare, and murder, during which he recognized no god but himself. In fact, murderers and other criminals are still buried in the specifically expressed "sure and certain hope of resurrection," as if postmortem punishment can be somehow waived by the same ecclesiastical authorities who created it and built their whole organization on an aggressively fostered public fear of it.

We might wonder why the annihilation threatened by the destructive Mother archetype should have seemed more frightening than the eternal pain threatened by the punitive Father. Why should the Goddess's death curse seem so terrible that man retreated from it into unrealistic denial, whereas the God's limitless torture chambers were believed in and accepted?

One reason might be that the Goddess, like Mother Maat, really did represent the truth. Whatever doctrines may receive their lip service, most people know at bottom that their God-given hells and heavens are fantasies, never seen and never seeable. On the other hand, the Goddess-given curse of death is all too real, verifiable by direct observation every day. We are never completely sure that the promise of heaven will be kept. But we know as sure as we have been born that the promise of death will be kept without exception. The "triumph over death," alleged and urged as a tenet of Christian faith, is not apparent in the real world.

Moreover, in actual practice we behave as if the promise of faith were never made at all. Fear of death is just as strong in the faithful as in those who believe it to be the final dissolution of the self. All grieve for dead loved ones, without any noticeable conviction that they are really still alive in some other place. Our behavior demonstrates that, for most people, faith in an afterlife is a verbal formality supposed to provide comfort in the face of death; yet when the veil of the terrible Crone is lifted at last, the comfort seems slight by comparison to the enormous effort of sustaining the belief against empirical evidence.

Perhaps as a result of such attempts to avoid the unavoidable, the faith that claimed to have conquered the Crone only succeeded in hiding her away in a charnel darkness that made her more terrible than ever. Consciously acknowledged or not, it was her image that really haunted the so-called Ages of Faith, rather than the somewhat friendlier—or at least more accessible—image of the devil. She had many guises: she-demon, witch, sorceress, succubus, Hag, Hecate, Lilith, Diana, Mara, Night-mare, Valkyrie, Wili, Fata Morgana, Lamia, Hel, Kraken, Banshee, Queen of the Shades. She became the secret fear of Western civilization, whose massive attempts to destroy her eventually sickened the society itself and poisoned its relationships between the sexes, in which man might have found real comfort and real courage to face the inevitable without forcing it prematurely upon his fellow creatures.

5

The Crone and the Cauldron

5

Shakespeare's three Weird Sisters, chanting over their cauldron, were direct descendants of the Triple Goddess Wyrd, or Weird (Fate), worshiped by Shakespeare's ancestors. More than eight centuries before the lifetime of the bard of Avon, the author of *Beowulf* revered the Goddess Wyrd who was also "the Word" (Wurd), writing the fate of every man in her book of life. She was another form of Eostre, the Easter Goddess said to have come from the land beyond the Ganges, that is, the home of Triple Kali, who also wrote each man's fate in her sacred Sanskrit letters.[1]

Similarly, the three Norns of Scandinavian myth were known as *Die Schreiberinnen,* "the Writing Women"; and Rome's Triple Goddess Fortuna was known as Fata Scribunda, "the Fate Who Writes."[2] Beowulf said the decrees of Wyrd were always final. Every man would have to bend his head reverently to her will.[3] In Greece the fatal female trinity controlled even the will of Zeus, who claimed paternal authority over all gods. According to Ovid, Fate was the Triple Goddess who "abhors boastful words," warning men to receive her edicts humbly, whether they brought good fortune or bad.[4] In the time of the Roman Empire, the Goddess Fate elicited "a passionate surrender" that has been compared to the eagerness of later Christian mystics to submit to the will of God.[5]

In the eleventh century A.D., Burchardus of Worms said people still honored the three Fates at the turn of the year, laying tables with food and drink for them, with three knives to cut the Three Sisters' meat.[6] In the twelfth century, the bishop of Exeter scolded those who laid tables with three knives for "the fairies" (fays, Fates), "that they may predestinate good to such as are born in the house."[7] Ecclesiastical disapproval notwithstanding, the Weird Sisters were recognized in Tudor England not only as witches, but also as the Fairy Godmothers who came to each infant's cradle "for to set to the babe what shall befall to him."[8] Gypsies never ceased to lay three pieces of bread on a baby's bed, "one for each Goddess of Fate."[9]

Why were the Wyrd/Weird Sisters, the Norns, the Fortunae, and other versions of the Triple Goddess so often associated with cauldrons?

Whatever Shakespeare may have said, the witch's cauldron seems to have been much more than a vessel for stewing newts' eyes, frogs' toes, or any other magical recipe. In the Middle Ages, the chief symbol standing in opposition to the male cross was the female cauldron. The vessel was an important and central symbol in pagan religion.

Variations on the northern Goddess Wyrd included Wurd (the Word) and Urd (Earth, Erda), whose "mighty roaring cauldron" lay deep at the root of the World Tree, that is to say at the foundation of the universe. It was tended by the Triple Goddess herself, in the shape of the Norns. This fount of life was sometimes known as Urdarbrunnr, the Stream of Urd.[10] The cauldron was usually described as the source of life, wisdom, inspiration, understanding, and magic. It might be likened to the ubiquitous "pot of blood" in the hand of Triple Kali, representing her primordial uterine Ocean of Blood that provided the original life energy for the creation.

Both Eastern and Western myths insisted that the aspiring Father God was obliged to steal his power and/or wisdom from some version of the Mother's vessel, before he could seriously claim domination over the world. Odin, the Aryan sky god, managed to drink the Wise Blood from three cauldrons in the womb of Earth (Erda), by tricking the "giantess" who tended them, and taking the sacred substance into himself when she wasn't looking. Thus illegally he acquired knowledge of reading and writing the runes, mastery of magic, shape-shifting ability, and understanding of cosmic matters, which were formerly the Goddess's exclusive property. When the myth was retold by patriarchal scribes in the Middle Ages, the Wise Blood in the cauldrons was said to be that of a male sacrificial victim called "Wisest of Men," a version of the story that harks back to the primitive sacrificial magic whereby men tried to approximate the child-making ability of women's wise blood by donating their own vital fluid to a symbolic womb, such as a cauldron.

In India, the sky god Indra also stole Wise Blood from Triple Kali's three cauldrons.[11] Vedic myths sometimes called it Soma, the mysterious essence of world-creating energy. Traced back to its original sources, Soma turns out to have been the Goddess's own lunar-menstrual fountain. It was red, it was associated with the moon, it created pregnancy, and it was the stuff of ongoing life and rebirth.

A worldwide cycle of myths reveals that the cauldron symbolized the cosmic mother-body, variously located in heaven, in the earth, in the sea, or at times in the moon. Babylonians said the dome of heaven was the lapis lazuli cauldron of the Fate Goddess Siris, "the wisewoman, the mother," who mingled the elements for generation and regeneration of living things.[12] The Egyptian hieroglyph that represented the Goddess of Creation, brooding over her own uterine Deep, was a design of three cauldrons above a water symbol.[13]

Mycenaean Demeter made a god of the sacrificial victim Pelops by resurrecting him from her magic cauldron.[14] This sort of magic was still attributed to the female trinity of Fate in the late Roman Empire, when the emperor Elagabalus declared himself "deified in the cauldron."[15] The same regenerative magic was performed by Demeter's Colchian counterpart Medea, who came into Hellenic myth as a mortal queen, but who was an eponymous Crone Mother of the Medes. Her name meant "Wisdom." She was known as an all-healer; our word *medicine* descended from her.[16] The classic writers wished to belittle her, so they ignored Herodotus's statement that she was the Great Goddess of all the Parthian Aryans.[17]

Male writers often tried to disguise earlier meanings of the cauldron and/or its contents, because these meanings would not serve the interests of patriarchies and emerging male-dominant religions. The image of the cosmic cauldron-as-womb proposed a source of creation that omitted the male principle. Later there was the theory held by many different peoples for a very long time, remnants of which are still in evidence today: that male creativity or divinity must depend on a fatal self-sacrifice, in order originally to replace the Mother's lunar blood in the cauldron with the blood of a male victim.

Obviously predating recognition of physiological paternity, this theory implied belief that only maternal blood was the life-giving essence. Therefore, the only way a male could participate in the Goddess's creative activity was to give his own blood to help replace what she used up. He was often rewarded with deification for this service, as ancient sacred kings were deified at the abrupt and violent termination of their allotted reigns. Still, such honors were deadly to the martyred heroes, who were perhaps not always as willing as propriety said they should have been. Even Jesus tried to escape the fate of sacred kingship before resigning himself to the offering of his blood (John 6:15).

Strabo mentioned gray-haired priestesses among the Cimbrian tribes, whose duty it was to pour the blood of sacrificed victims into their sacred cauldrons, while they read omens in the entrails.[18] Still extant is the famous Gundestrup cauldron, an Iron Age ceremonial vessel perhaps of Cimbrian origin. On its sides, figures in relief show a line of male victims advancing on foot, to be plunged by a giant priest, priestess, or deity into a double-lobed yoni-gate, guarded by the usual death dog, the Crone's familiar. Above, the victims depart crowned, on horseback, which meant death and apotheosis, to take their places in heaven.

A similar scene on a cista from Palestrina-Praeneste shows the pre-Roman Mars, a sacrificial fertility god of the Ides of March, naked and kneeling before the boiling cauldron, to be pushed down into it by the Wisdom Goddess Minerva. She was the Latin form of Athene, called Menarva the Crone by the Etruscans. She was accompanied as usual by her ever-present, gate-guarding dog, three-headed Cerberus.[19]

In Persian scriptures, another version of the same Wise Goddess escorted the soul of a hero or sage into paradise, appearing to him as the divine lady "of high understanding," the lady "who can discern," with her dogs alongside her.[20] Dogs were first domesticated by women, the food givers; and canine territorial instinct made the dog the first animal guardian of woman's hearth and home place. Hence there was always a close mythical relationship between the Goddess and her carrion-eating canine familiars. During Renaissance witch persecutions, dogs were cited even more than cats as the companions of witches.[21]

Up to modern times, shamans of central Asia and Siberia believed a rite of the cauldron symbolically essential to the enlightenment (or apotheosis) of a heroic sage. To become a shaman, a man must be killed by the spirits of his ancestors and boiled in a magic cauldron until reduced to bare bones. Then he must be "reborn" as the bones are given new flesh. Some said a true shaman must boil in the cauldron for three years. The very word *shaman* (Tunguistic *saman*) means "One Who Has Died," derived from the Aryan god Samana, Lord of Death. In Tibetan Tantrism, enlightened souls were those who experienced death and rebirth in vivid dreams, where they entered an iron cauldron, called the House of Iron or the Iron Mountain, and were dismembered by *rakshasas* (demonic spirits), boiled, and restored to life. Afterward, they were viewed as survivors of a vitally important initiatory ordeal.[22]

Sacred cauldrons continued to figure in the remnants of pagan custom that came to be called witchcraft during Europe's Middle Ages. Salic law named certain witches Hereburge, that is, dwellers on the Mount of the Goddess Hera; they were said to carry the copper cauldron to their places of enchantment.[23] A few of the ancient sacred vessels survived up to the modern era. Frensham Church in Surrey preserved "an extraordinary great kettle or cauldron" supposedly donated by the fairies.[24] Since the terms for fairies and witches were interchangeable, and both were called fays, fates, or *fatidae,* they were obviously based on the "fatal women" who were once priestesses of the Goddess.

What Christian tradition most assiduously concealed was not the sacramental use of the cauldron, but its theological meaning in the old religions. Like any symbol of vast antiquity, it had acquired complex and far-reaching interpretations through the millenia.

Always the cauldron was understood to signify the cosmic womb, source of regeneration and rebirth. All life, mind, matter, and energy arose in various forms from the ever-boiling vessel, only to return thereto, when each form came to its destined end. As ingredients dissolved and mingled in boiling, so the elements that made all things were separated and recombined in the cauldron: so ran the basic theory. As the Christian cross stood for linear finality—one death, one resurrection, one postmortem reward (or punishment) forever—so the pagan cauldron stood for its opposite, perpetual cyclic recurrence.

Sometimes the cauldron represented the Great Mother herself. One of the Celtic maternal trinity (the Morrigan) was Babd, the Boiling One, corresponding to the Mother or Preserver figure of Kali as the primal "Ocean of Blood."[25] Sometimes this same primal ocean was made of the other maternal fluid, milk; its boiling or churning produced everything in the universe. India, Japan, Egypt, Persia, and Homeric Greece had comparable myths of cosmic creation out of the "incomparably mighty" churning of a milky sea, which curdled in the same way that blood might clot, to give birth to continents and other solid objects.[26]

Several pagan traditions likened the cauldron-womb to a kind of impeller for the eternally churning ocean, locating it in an enchanted place beneath the sea, where the dead went in the kind of sea burial that Vikings called "returning to the Mother's womb."[27] This "mighty roaring cauldron," churn, quern, or mill ground out all things in its constant activity, making enormous whirlpools in the sea, and all the phenomena of waves and tides.

The Norse legend of the Maelstrom (Mill-Stream) placed the primary vortex in the Western ocean, in the direction of the pagan paradise, which was usually supposed to be an island presided over by the Goddess herself, as the Morrigan, Morgan, Fairy Queen, Freya, Hel, and so on. Celts located their divine Cauldron of Regeneration in the land-beneath-the-waves, or else on the magic Apple-land (Avalon) over the Western sea.[28]

The extreme antiquity of the concept is indicated by its many interpretations, worked on by many people throughout the Eurasian continent, and the many places or objects with which the cauldron has been identified.

All over Britain, even Christians continued to worship ancient holy wells and springs, especially those in earth-womb caves, or those whose waters bubbled and boiled like seething cauldrons, because their pagan ancestors had regarded such places as healing shrines. They were so regarded because ancient people thought them earthly manifestations of the cosmic womb, where all life could be endlessly regenerated. The Christian habits of well dressing, offering money to certain honored waters, and annually "taking the waters" of allegedly medicinal springs, descended from pagan worship of the regenerative womb as it was envisioned in many kinds of natural phenomena.

One of the most famous healing shrines was Bath, once sacred to the Goddess Sulis: a Gaelic title of the Great Mother meaning "the eye," or "the hole," from *Suil*, an all-seeing eye, an eye in the sense of an orifice, like the eye of a grommet, the eye of a storm, or the eye of a whirlpool. An Icelandic term for a whirlpool was related to the same source, also the English word *swallow.* The word implied both the Goddess's devouring Hole, and her far-sightedness and propetic wisdom; we recall that in the East, the Goddess's genital yoni was sometimes also a symbol of an eye. Sulis was the same Mother Earth whose gigantic tumulus-womb was raised at Silbury Hill. Her naturally boiling cauldron in the earth at Bath was a pilgrimage center for thousands of years before Christians seized it, "an oracular 'Otherworld' cult centre, under the power of a Celtic or pre-Celtic Mother Goddess."[29]

Finnish mythology presents an amalgam of Asian and European pagan ideas of the cosmic womb. It is a cauldron, a quern, or a mill called Sampo, once located either in the earth or in the sea, "nine fathoms deep," under the jurisdiction of the Crone of Pohja. Some said it was kept in the Mount of Copper, recalling Aphrodite's Copper Isle, Cyprus, where she appeared in Crone form as Moira, "Fate," a trinity older than Time. Plutarch identified her with the underground Isis, called Nephthys, with the titles of Victory and Finality, also known as "the One Who Is All."[30] As the "Dark Aphrodite" of the north, she gave her name of Skadi, or Scotia, to Scotland.[31] Copper was sacred to her in northern lands as well as in the Greco-Roman world.

The Sampo kept at the Mount of Copper was said to produce all the world's food, and other necessities. The Book of Fate could be read in its "pictured cover," perhaps meaning the starry heavens. A primary Finnish myth cycle is concerned with the loss of the Sampo, which somehow withdrew to a misty island far away, a land of eternal peace, as "fairy tales" often pictured the matriarchal paradise. As a reminiscence of the peace-loving agricultural societies before patriarchal invasions brought war and pillage, this magic Isle of the Sampo—or, the cauldron of regeneration—was "where they eat not and they fight not, whither swordsmen never wander."[32]

The gods themselves initiated a desperate quest for the lost vessel, but it was never found. Therefore, the well-being of former ages was never restored. This is the central theme of European folklore, recognizable in many sources.

The Finns maintained their paganism throughout the Middle Ages, though their beliefs were forbidden by Christian authorities, and Christian kings forbade their subjects to travel to Finland to consult the local witches. The Finns persisted in saying the world was created by a female deity, and "mothers" were the agents of rebirth and resurrection, even of gods.[33] Such ideas were clearly opposed to Christianity, which recognized only male deities, and through its endless Crusades and conquests sought to substitute the phallic cross for the uterine cauldron.

Paganism went underground, and took the cauldron with it. Nearly every European country inherited hidden legends of a lost miraculous vessel, the source of life or of enlightenment. The Finns' Sampo was only one of its manifestations. Christian mysticism tried to assimilate another, the Celtic Cauldron of Regeneration, disguised as the Holy Grail. Ultimately, such attempts failed, as the Grail quest itself failed. Though the church initially encouraged literary adoption and elaboration of the legend, the whole vision was soon abandoned. Scholars knew all too well the original sources and meanings of the Grail. The poets of early medieval Europe also knew the blood-filled vessel of life energy was the cauldron of the Crone long before it was the cup of Christ.

One of the greatest of these poets, Taliesin, claimed to have received his inspiration directly from the cauldron of the Crone herself, his own divine mother Cerridwen, one of the old names for the cauldron's custodian. Like her Greek, Roman, and Egyptian counterparts, Cerridwen was a devourer of the dead, and a giver of rebirth. In a sense, the Cauldron was herself. Her body produced life, wisdom, and inspiration: according to pre-Christian belief, the divine attributes of female uterine blood.

These attributes Cerridwen boiled in her cauldron for a year and a day: the matriarchal calendar of thirteen lunar months plus one day. Finally she was able to distill three precious drops of the Grace of Inspiration for her son.[34] His inspired poetry spoke of the Cauldron from which proceeded the Word (Wyrd), hidden in the mystic "revolving castle" at the hub of the turning universe, which others envisioned in many ways: the mill, the maelstrom, the eye, the *axis mundi,* the omphalos, or the Goddess's life-giving genital center.[35]

This turning, churning vessel was transformed into the first Christian symbol that could be found to resemble it, the Eucharistic cup, which was likewise filled with blood/wine. Clergymen took over the old pagan shrine of Glastonbury, formerly an omphalos centered on the sacred "Blood Spring," and declared it the new home of the cup from which Christ and his disciples drank at the Last Supper—even though this cup was never seen on the premises.[36]

A complex series of tales appeared, to explain the transportation of the cup from the Holy Land by Joseph of Arimathea and a group of his friends, who installed it in the shrine after several miracles arranged by God, to demonstrate his will in his usual elliptical manner. Afterward, the cup mysteriously disappeared. Some said that, even after going to all that trouble and staging all those miracles, God had changed his mind about entrusting so valuable a relic to mere mortals, and had removed it to heaven. At the same time, other tales located the Grail in a holy castle in the Pyrenees, attended by sacred maidens and ruled by a mystic queen; or in Caer Sidi, the revolving castle somewhere underground; or in some version of fairyland.

Not every story gave the Holy Grail an unequivocally Christian origin. Some Christian writers claimed it was made of a jewel that fell from the crown of Lucifer, the Lapis Exilis or Phoenix Stone, which like the ancient cauldron was credited with power to renew youth. Alternatively, it was called Theolithus, the magic stone with the power of "inexhaustible feeding," like the womb of Earth herself.[37]

Female sexual symbolism was never wholly expunged from the Grail stories. In many instances, the vessel was accompanied by the holy lance, or spear, traditional emblem of the Goddess's phallic consorts, some of whom were transformed into Lancelot (Big Lance), Peredur, Percival, Galahad, and other Grail knights. In its legendary processions, the Grail was carried by a maiden, the lance by a youth. Christian exegetes claimed the lance was the same one that pierced Christ's side, wielded by the mythical Saint Longinus. However, the Grail and lance were recognizably "sex symbols of immemorial antiquity and world wide diffusion."[38]

Christian writers of Grail myths impaled themselves on the horns of a dilemma when they tried to explain the mysterious urgency of the great quest. If the chalice in every church was literally the cup of Christ's blood, as the authorities officially claimed, then Christian knights would hardly need to ride to the ends of the earth in search of it. By the orthodox reasoning, the world was already saved through the sacrifice and transubstantiation to which the church laid exclusive title. If found in real life, the Grail would have been no more than another relic, like thousands already celebrated all over Christendom: pieces of the true cross, pieces of Mary's veil, Saint Luke's paintings, apostles' hair, shreds of the crucifixion robe, the crown of thorns, the nails, the aforementioned lance, and every other conceivable bit of hardware associated with the sacrifice. And yet, ahead of all other such articles, the Grail seems to have been sought with almost feverish intensity, as if the fate of the world somehow hung in the balance.

The urgency of the Grail quest is explicable only with reference to its pagan symbolism. Christianized versions of the story soon petered out and were forgotten so abruptly as to suggest conscious suppression. Jessie Weston says, "We can now understand why the Church knows nothing of the Grail; why that Vessel, surrounded as it is with an atmosphere of reverence and awe, equated with the central sacrament of the Christian Faith, yet appears in no Legendary, is figured in no picture, comes on the scene in no Passion Play. The Church of the eleventh and twelfth centuries knew well what the Grail was, and we . . . need no longer wonder why a theme, for some short space so famous and so fruitful a source of literary inspiration, vanished utterly and completely from the world of literature."[39]

Neither need we wonder why the Grail's literary disappearance coincided with the period of consolidation of intellectual and political power in the hands of the church, which came to control education and literacy. During this period, virtually nothing was written at all, unless it was written by clergymen. Even most accounts of historical events in these centuries have been filtered down through ecclesiastical reporters, whose objectivity was minimal at best, since they always served their organization's purposes first.

What was it that the twelfth-century churchmen knew about the Grail, which rendered it ultimately unacceptable as a Christian symbol and led to its obliteration by the church's censors? It can hardly be doubted that some churchmen, at least, understood the secret identity of the Grail with the pagans' Cauldron of Regeneration, still represented in the observances of so-called witches, who were known to revere the female principle above any masculine

God or savior, and for whom old women were figures of spiritual authority. The Crone and the ever-churning cosmic womb were mirrored on earth by the old priestess or wisewoman and her boiling cauldron. This was one reason for the church's five-century campaign against old women, millions of whom met torture and fiery death at the hands of "God's gestapo."

Another reason for the suppression of the Grail was the obvious incompatibility between Christian theology and that of its pagan rivals, which not only worshiped a female deity (or deities), but also opposed the whole Christian system of postmortem reward and punishment. The Cauldron/Grail represented cycles and recurrences, not linear heaven-or-hell choices made once for all time.

The Grail myths themselves hint that the urgency of the quest sprang from a belief that the orthodox religion was wrong. The myths prophesied that without the beneficent influence of the Grail (or cauldron), Europeans would become alienated from the principle of fertility, and bring on the terrible condition known as *la Terre Gast,* "the Waste Land."

This belief might be traced to those Eastern lands that had been most recently taken over by a patriarchal religion, Islam, after thousands of years of female leadership and Goddess worship, documented as far back as the seventh century B.C.[40] Followers of Mohammed had begun the violent imposition of a male-dominant religious and social system on Arabia only four centuries before the first Crusades brought them into contact and conflict with Europeans. Arabian Goddess worship was not yet dead. Wars, pilgrimages, and conquest of European-held fiefs in and around the Holy Land eventually triggered the Renaissance, by exposing Europeans to Eastern science and culture. They learned some of the ideas of Sufi mystics and others who still maintained reverence for the female principle. European Cabalists, Hermetists, and troubadours of the "romantic" or "courtly love" movements drew much of their philosophy from such mystics.

Some European thinkers adopted the Eastern mystics' despairing explanation for the barrenness of Arabia Deserta, the lifeless desert. The literal meaning of a desert is "that which has been deserted." Some Sufis and Shi'ites claimed their land had been deserted by the Goddess because of Islam's demonstrations of contempt for the female principle, the true source of life and fertility; without her, nothing could flourish. Ibn El-Arabi, the "greatest master" of Sufi mystics, insisted that the supreme deity was female, even though his Mohammedan opponents accused him of blasphemy.[41]

Arabian mystics yearned for the coming of the savior they called the Mahdi or moon-guided one, to be born of a virgin named Paradise by the Goddess's grace, to restore love and fertility to the blasted land. In Europe, this personage became the Desired Knight of the Grail myth cycle.

European travelers viewed Arabia Deserta with horror. Some of them related its lifeless condition to centuries-old warning prophecies from their own pre-Christian traditions. They thought if the seasonal rites of the Great Mother were neglected, a similar fate might fall on the fertile lands of Europe. Yet the Christian church, by insisting on abandonment of the old ways, risked exactly such a fate. Might not the Goddess in her anger desert the Western countries she had so long sustained? Certain groups of so-called witches probably were trying to prevent their own land's suffering the same fate that afflicted desert places in the East, where men foolishly defied the wrath of the Mother.

Thus, there was an amalgam of Eastern mysticism and pagan oracular tradition in the Grail myths, before their forced reinterpretation by Christian exegetes. The latter versions were wholly artificial. Certainly there was no actual carrying of Christ's cup to Glastonbury, or anywhere else, by Joseph of Arimathea; there was no search for the same cup by Christian knights; there was no real Grail any more than there was a real Cauldron. In effect, the story was a battle of symbols.

Modern scholarship inherits the problem of reconstructing the battle by deduction and inference. We no longer know for sure what the symbols stood for. Their meanings have been erased from our collective consciousness. We know the basic world view of the winner, that is, male-dominated Judeo-Christianity. But we have little information about the theology of Europe's pagans and heretics, not only because the people themselves were destroyed, but also because their literature, oral traditions, customs, and sacred histories were destroyed wherever possible.

Some items, it is true, "fell through the cracks" of persecution, and were hidden in unlikely places, such as doggerel rhymes, nursery tales, carnival games, folk festivals, songs, dances, and superstitions. Most of these were scraps of ritual. Once, behind the rituals, there had been a coherent philosophy. The church had found this philosophy so inimical to its own, that it had allowed itself to be guilty of a thousand years of relentless warfare, and five more centuries of mass murder, to rid the earth of its rivals.

We must discover what the cauldron meant.

The symbol itself reveals much. Endlessly churning, endlessly turning, a boiling matrix, a soup of elemental raw materials in the cosmic womb, the cauldron represented the stuff of creation, the Mother's "eternal flux." As depicted in the Bible, deprived of its female personification, it was "the Deep," *tehom,* which the Egyptians called the primal being, Temu, and the Babylonians knew as All-Mother Tiamat. Jewish scribes also called it (or her) Chaos, Formlessness, or *tohu bohu.* This came in a direct line from Goddess worshipers beyond the Ganges, who described the All-Mother as existing in the state of "dark formlessness" between universes, when she rested from the constant labor of creating, and allowed all things to be dissolved into their component elements until she began creating again.[42]

The cauldron symbolized creation that occurred not just once, as in the Bible story, but constantly, as long as the universe lasted. It represented the Goddess power that formed every child in the womb, every plant in its seed, every bird, fish, reptile, or insect in its egg: the life force, Nature, or Being, all of which were alternate names for the Goddess herself. Everything was created in her, and returned to her "at the time of dissolution," according to her "fatal" or "karmic" laws.[43]

The Goddess's worshipers viewed themselves as inextricably in and of the living environment, cousin to animals and plants, wind and water, in the churning elemental cauldron of nature. A human being lived only for a short space. Soon he would die, dissolve into his component atoms, and become something else. The same fate overtook even the gods, who also dissolved into the eternal flux.

In India, Kali's uterine cauldron or "pot of blood" represented her creative power, and also the flux or formless Deep between the destruction of each universe and the creation of the next. Holding within herself all elements of existence before they were combined into living forms, she constantly broke down forms and rebuilt them, always destroying and creating, without beginning or end. Everything returned in its time to her churning womb. As it was said of one of her Middle Eastern counterparts, Astarte, "the true sovereign of the world," she created and destroyed in tireless activity, eliminating what had lived out its time, and bringing forth the new.[44] The later gods who claimed to be "without beginning and without end" actually copied the idea from older scriptures of the Goddess, whose worshipers declared that the only true magic of creation was necessarily found in the image of motherhood, since only mothers could bring forth new life.

The cauldron concept of eternally recycling life was inevitably opposed to the patriarchal linear concept, evinced by such male-dominated groups as Jain Buddhists, Mithraic Persians, Essenic Jews, and orthodox Christians. According to the visions shared by such groups, each life passed only once from birth to death, and, if human, must face a postmortem judgment by which to be saved or damned. The pious would go to heaven (Nirvana) and remain forever in a changeless state. The wicked would go to eternal punishment. As it evolved into the sadistic Christian hell, this infinite punishment seemed rather excessive for the trivial sins of one brief lifetime; but the theologians nevertheless insisted that the results of the final judgment would never be rescinded. There could be no recycling, no reincarnation, no turning of the karmic wheel, no resorption of the soul into any inchoate mass of universal soul-stuff. Patriarchal religions narrowed the focus to the self alone, regarding all the rest of the universe as mere backdrop for the miniscule drama of man's salvation, played out upon its vast stage.

The idea that each self was only a temporary offshoot of an all-embracing, motherly World Soul (Shakti) was anathema to patriarchal thinkers. It could only make nonsense of their system of postmortem reward and punishment. The church's political and economic supremacy in Europe was upheld, ultimately, by the carrot-and-stick combination of fears of hell and hopes for heaven. To remove heaven and hell from the vision would be to treat all soul-stuff alike, as the Orientals did, making little or no distinction between the pious and the wicked, human and animal, We and They. It would sever the reins of guilt, fear, and shame whereby priests controlled the laity. It could foster another version of Eastern pantheistic, female-centered worship of nature, thus bringing on the downfall of a church founded on the premise of female sinfulness and exclusively male divinity.

Perhaps that was why Christian churches accused "witches" of seeking to destroy the kingdom of God on earth. Under no circumstances would the theologians share God's kingdom with a Goddess, even though the common people often did so by implication, calling her by the name of Mary. To recognize the feminine principle in religion meant a broader, less elitist view of others and of the whole natural creation, perhaps implicit in the very psychology of men and women. Recent studies have shown that men tend to be concerned about their own self-perpetuation and personal immortality, while women think less of self and more of relationship. If women envision a personal afterlife, it is in terms of reunion with their loved ones.[45]

Accordingly, female-centered societies usually reverenced the principle of matrilineal kinship on the personal and the universal scale simultaneously. Nature was a Mother who birthed them all and who would take them back. The environment was literally the same as the ancestors worshiped as clan divinities. Having been returned to the matrix, as it were, their very substance became soil, grass, water, food, other creatures.

People like the American Indians drew no rigid lines between human life and the life of the environment, as did the Christians, who decided that nature was wholly "inanimate" and existed only for the use of *man*kind, attributing this arrangement to a God who was not part of the world he made, but existed outside of it. The Indians' view was that Mother Earth and all her children were one. In the very process of living, they constantly interchanged their substance with her. They believed the Mother would produce sufficient nourishment for the needs of every creature, provided her gifts were never abused by human greed. It was a moral principle that one should not take more than necessary from Nature's bounty. Conservation of resources was an essential part of a religion largely shaped by women. To offend their Mother Earth was to risk her rejection. After death, such an offender could never experience another rebirth from her all-embracing womb.[46]

Modern feminists, conscious of contemporary environmental problems, strongly criticize the patriarchal tendency to disconnect and compartmentalize "man" and "nature." From such compartmentalization arose the doctrines that matter and spirit are inimical opposites, that only men have souls, and that human beings must be isolated from the environment even in death. Rosemary Radford Ruether points out that a more realistic acceptance of death, like that of the Crone worshipers, would achieve a new identification with "the larger matrix" as a living entity that contains and supports the human species along with every other. "To bury ourselves in steel coffins, so that we cannot disintegrate into the earth, is to refuse to accept this process of entering back into the matrix of renewed life. Such a manner of burial represents a fundamental refusal to accept earth as our home and the plants and animals of earth as our kindred."[47]

In antiquity, the cauldron stood for the larger matrix. The beginnings of the atomic theory, cut off in Europe's Dark Ages and revived only in our own century, clearly pointed to the cyclic concept of nature, life, and death. About 60 B.C., Lucretius wrote in *On the Nature of Things:*

> No single thing abides, but all things flow.
> Fragment to fragment clings; the things thus grow
> Until we know and name them. By degrees
> They melt, and are no more the things we know.
> Globed from the atoms, falling slow or swift
> I see the suns, I see the systems lift
> Their forms; and even the systems and their suns
> Shall go back slowly to the eternal drift.[48]

This poem could have been written by a twentieth-century scientist; its imagery does no particular violence to our present understanding of the cosmos. Still, such imagery was forbidden to European minds a few centuries after Lucretius, when pagan ideas of time cycles, reincarnation, and consecutive universes were anathematized as opposed to the true faith.

At this point the symbol of the cauldron was lost, and never developed further. It began to disintegrate into a thousand half-remembered, fragmentary notions, sayings, incantations, hidden rites, and heretical whispers. Once the church declared itself the final repository of truth, no further pursuit of truth in either discussion or experimentation was to be allowed.

However, alternative methods of seeking enlightenment were not altogether abandoned. The rich complexity and hoary age of pagan tradition was not to be erased in only a few centuries. The patriarchal theology simplistically ignored one entire half of the living world, the female half: the more important half, as related to the life of the future. Even when they dared not say it, women knew in their blood that femaleness was more essential to life than was the God who had called femaleness accursed. Some men knew it too. Of these, some devised other ways of dealing symbolically with the female principle, in mystical or esoteric studies, largely hidden from ecclesiastical eyes.

One such study developed into alchemy. Alchemists had their own version of the cauldron, a round or egg-shaped vessel variously called *vas mirabile, vas spirituale,* or *vas Hermetis,* "a kind of matrix or uterus." The vessel was said to be filled with the red *elixir vitae* (fluid of life), *panacea,* or *prima materia,* the primal *mater* (mother) of *mater*ial or matter. The alchemists' goal was to release this mysterious all-producing entity from the bonds of "dead" matter. This was defined as a bringing-to-birth, out of the mystic waters in which all things are contained—recalling ancient images like that of Mother Tiamat, who was defined as "Waters." The offspring, called Glorious Child, Perfect Body, or *filius macrocosmi* (Son of the Universe), was either the anima (soul) of the world, or the wonderful Philosopher's Stone, ruler of the elements.[49] There were correspondences between this strange entity and the stone of which the Grail was supposed to have been made.

The alchemists' "son of the philosophers" might be likened to the Mahdi, who was credited by Arabian alchemists with the power of enlightenment, or to the Messiah, the Desired Knight, and the expected second Christ in European tradition. Alchemy was the special study of Arabian mystics before it came to Europe. Some of its most famous early practitioners were said to have been female. In Arabic, *al-khemeia* meant "a science from the land of the moon," after Khemennu, "Land of the Moon," an ancient name for Egypt.[50]

East or West, alchemists were not concerned with chemical research in the modern sense. They had no concept of chemical research in the modern sense. They believed their manipulations with retorts and flasks would show them the transcendental secrets of Nature herself. Therefore, their discipline was known as natural science, meaning literally knowledge of Nature. Like many before them, the alchemists yearned to gaze on the serpent-wreathed countenance of Medusa the Wise, and live to tell the tale.

Their chosen guide to the secrets of Nature was Hermes Trismegistus, "Thrice-Great Hermes," the god who once lived as the original hermaphrodite in the same body with the Goddess Aphrodite, and was therefore privy to her secrets. The alchemical *vas* was often called the "womb" of Hermes, "a uterus for spiritual renewal or rebirth." Alchemists actually compared it to the Grail. An alchemical treatise of the sixteenth century said this vessel was "more to be sought than scripture."[51]

In pagan times, Hermes was worshiped at crossroads throughout the Roman empire, together with the Crone aspect of his female half, Hecate, the "most lovely one," who was sometimes a trinity in her own right, identified with the moon, and later adopted by Christian Europe as the Queen of the Ghostworld or Queen of Witches.[52] Occasionally Hecate was given as the collective name of the feminine trinity of Selene, the Moon, ruler of heaven; Artemis or Diana, the Huntress, ruler of earth; and Persephone, the Destroyer, ruler of the underworld.[53] Originally, she was the Egyptian Crone-midwife-matriarch Hekat or Heqit, vessel of female wisdom *(heq),* who could reveal the secrets of nature. She knew the ways of all hidden things, such as the fetus in the womb, which the Egyptians totemically represented by her sacred animal, the frog. Romans also believed frogs especially favored by the Goddess.

Medieval Europe still maintained the connection between frogs and the Crone–midwife–witch-queen. It was claimed that every frog was the reincarnation of an infant who died unbaptized, or of an aborted fetus.[54] The church insisted that any such infant was automatically damned to an eternity of suffering, but pagan wise-women of northern Europe gave it a kinder fate. They said the unbaptized baby would be gently received by the underground Goddess, Hel or Frau Holde, their own counterpart of Hecate, whose subterranean realm was not like the Christian hell of eternal torture.[55] Women were understandably disgusted by the Christian

God's cruelty toward newborn infants, which really arose from the Oedipal hostilities of the men who made God's rules for him.

Many pagans regarded the Moon Mother as a primary receiver of souls, which she recycled as her star-children, giving them astral ("starry") bodies while they dwelt in heaven. Hecate was assimilated to this image also. She was not only the underworld ruler; she was also the moon. The three faces that she showed as Hecate Triformis were said to be the three phases of the moon: the waxing Maiden, the full Mother, the waning Crone.[56]

Such ancient ideas were united in the alchemical Goddess, shown in the texts as a naked female Luna (Moon), joining a naked male Sol (Sun); or as an Aphroditean mermaid rising crowned from the sea; or as a celestial Virgo; or as the pre-Hellenic "Mistress of Earth and Sea" with one foot on land and the other in the ocean; or as Isis, Diana, Juno, or Eve. All these and still other names for the Goddess recurred in alchemical texts. In such ways did alchemy preserve a symbolic sort of Goddess worship while the prevailing orthodoxy anathematized it. Alchemists said nothing could work properly without the female power, who bluntly told her male consort that he was helpless without her, "as a cock is helpless without a hen."[57]

A common name of the alchemical Goddess was a classic epithet of the Crone: Sapientia, the Lady Wisdom, a Latinized version of the early Gnostic-Christian Great Mother Sophia, "Wisdom." Before she was declared a heretical aberration by the emerging orthodoxy of the sixth century, Sophia reigned in Constantinople's greatest church, and figured in Gnostic gospels as the admonisher and correcter of Jehovah, having the natural authority of his Mother. She was a trinity, known by three names, "although She exists alone, since She is perfect." In the *Trimorphic Protennoia*, she said: "I am the Womb that gives shape to the All by giving birth to the Light that shines in splendor. I am the Aeon to come. I am the fulfilment of the All, that is, Meirothea, the glory of the Mother. I cast a Sound of the Voice into the ears of those who know me."[58] Medieval alchemists considered themselves members of the elite group of those who knew her.

Alchemical texts preserved the trinity of Sapientia as Creatress, Disposer, and Governor of the world, its being, light, and life, "the basic and primordial foundation of all things."[59] They said she "wears the royal crown of seven glittering stars . . . and on her robe is written in golden lettering, in Greek, Arabic, and Latin: I am the only daughter of the wise, utterly unknown to the foolish." She said: "Come ye to me and be enlightened, and your operations shall not be confounded."[60]

Alchemists dealt with the female principle in ways that could have been called heretical, had they been plainly stated. But alchemical books seldom stated anything plainly. They were filled with allegories, secret codes, anagrams, number magic, astrological arcana, and mystical symbols designed to shut out the uninitiated. This may explain why alchemists usually escaped the attentions of the Inquisition, while witches didn't. Also, most alchemists were male and fairly well-to-do (their books and equipment were costly), while most witches were female and poor. Up to a point, the church tolerated heretical activity as an avocation of wealthy men, or even clerics, some of whom dabbled in "natural science." It would not tolerate any such intellectual endeavors on the part of women.

During this period of history, Crone and cauldron underwent several transformations. She continued to represent the principle of wisdom. Her vessel continued to represent the source of life, mind, and the cosmic order. But she was revered only in secret. In general, Christianity diabolized her. As a symbol, she was cut off from the reality of women, especially elder women, her *eidolons* who were once looked up to as oracles, arbiters of law, and vessels of the "wise blood" that knew the mysteries of existence. The Grail quest failed to find her. The alchemists failed to understand her. And the Waste Land came indeed—not yet on the face of the earth, but certainly within the human spirit, where all symbols really live.

It has been seen that autocratic male-dominated religions tend to assume preeminence during hard times, when deities seem unkind, and many people despair of improving their lot in life. Christianity found its initial impetus in a Roman Empire that was breaking down amid "a brooding consciousness of failure," prey to gloomy thoughts about the heavy weight of human sins, and the consequent anger of gods.[61] Similar widespread hopelessness and alienation marked the onset of the witch persecutions in a Europe decimated by the Black Death and disappointed by the failure of its Crusades in the Holy Land, which did not enrich the Western world as they had been expected to do.

The cross, symbol of painful death, obliterated the cauldron, symbol of churning life—even though both were envisioned by their worshipers as instruments of death followed by resurrection. The essential distinction between these symbols was their male-female polarity.

Rigid, unyielding, linear, the cross symbolized a death dictated by the autocratic Father who would have no other gods before him, and whose allegedly "dearly beloved" Son was supposed to offer up his life as obediently as a soldier following pseudopaternal orders on a battlefield. The cross stood for the younger man's abject subordination to the paternal will, in the hope of atoning for a crime that someone else committed: in other words, for a massive, objectless sense of guilt. Teaching their world that every person was born guilty of original sin, through the mere fact of having been born of woman, the Heavenly Father's priests blamed all the world's woes on man—or, more precisely, on woman. They failed to notice that they were in effect ceding to mere humanity the power to overrule God's purported desire for universal goodness, and forcing mere humanity to accept the punishment due the devil.

By contrast, the Crone's cauldron had no linear or hierarchical form. Like Arthur's Round Table, its shape obliterated rank. Its eternally mingling contents did away with separations of sheep from goats, saved from damned, We from They. All were one in the Mother.

Even the Mother herself, as perpetual shapeshifter, assumed the forms of all living things as well as the totality of the living world. Her Crone body was always retransformed into the birth-giving Virgin, as Persephone became the Kore, and Mari-Ishtar became Mary, the *almah* or "Maiden" of the Hebrew Bible. This feminine transformational magic is seen in several matriarchal figures even in the Bible. Sarah, "the Queen," conceived and bore her child at the ripe Crone age of ninety (Gen. 17:17). Elizabeth conceived John the Baptist in her old age (Luke 1:36). Such details show that even patriarchal writers thought the inner wise blood of post-menopausal women could still perform its regenerative miracle.

As Babd the Boiling One, the triple Morrigan, or the Welsh

Modron (Mother), otherwise known as Cerridwen or Morgan, the Celtic Crone too slipped easily from one form to another, old witch to Virgin, Destroyer to Creator. Morgan was sometimes a hag, sometimes a beautiful girl. She mothered the god Mabon, the hero Owein, and other pagan celebrities.

Geoffrey of Monmouth believed in her actual existence as the leader of "nine enchantresses" on the secret Western paradise Isle of Avalon or fairyland. These sacred women knew all the arts of healing, alchemical transformations, and how to fly through the air. In the form of Sena (modern Sein), this isle existed in the Western sea off the Breton coast, where the nine "white-haired" priestesses continued to rule almost up to modern times. Local legend never ceased to credit these nine old women with the ability to heal, to predict the future, to transform themselves into different shapes, and to control the weather.[62]

There is little doubt that certain hereditary matriarchal colonies survived, with traditions of Goddess worship and cauldron imagery, even in a Europe dominated by an all-male church and swept by the perpetual skirmishings of might-is-right militarism. As Fairy Queen, seeress, healer, necromancer, or sybil, the Crone remained hidden away in her sacred cave, barrow, mountain, grove, or island, officially outlawed, but still commanding the attention, the hopes, and the fears of common people. Her priestesses continued to invoke her whenever God declined to answer their prayers. Some such invocations have survived, addressing the Triple Goddess as "three sisters of fairies" or "Sibylia," quaintly conjuring her by God the Father, God the Son, and God the "Holieghost," to reveal treasures hidden in the earth, to provide good counsel, or to give the suppliant rings of invisibility and similar favors.[63]

Celtic traditions also tell of medieval "fairy" (pagan) women who married Christian men, indicating that, at least in some areas, there was a women's religion distinct from Christianity. In Ireland there were some separate cemeteries for men and women, suggesting separate burial rites, therefore originally separate clergy. Women's burial grounds could "never be entered by a living woman or a dead man."[64] Welsh fairy wives were said to follow matriarchal rules: they owned all the household goods and cattle, and would not tolerate marital abuse as Christian wives did. If a husband struck his fairy wife once (or, in some stories, three times), she would vanish, taking her property with her.[65]

It was precisely such independent, property-owning wives who were defined as witches by the Inquisition at the outset of persecution, which apparently succeeded in destroying the last vestiges of matriarchal tradition and law, leaving Europe's women exposed to a type of marriage that amounted to sexual and economic enslavement. Even the time-honored custom of bride price was done away with, and husbands were allowed to acquire not only the wife but also her property, as dowry.

Christianized Europe changed the image of the mysterious old unmarried wisewoman who used to guard the Grail castle, who once stood for high priestesshood, and for sole female access to the secret Holy of Holies in shrines that were hidden from men. She reappeared in some romances as the Grail messenger, a Crone form of the lily maid (Virgin) Elaine; but she was known as the Loathly Damsel. Germanic poems presented her as an emblem of sin. Chrétien de Troyes said she was "a damsel more hideous than could be pictured outside of hell."[66]

Patriarchal society often views physical ugliness as the worst of sins in a female, overriding all compensatory qualities of virtue, kindness, or intelligence, because these qualities are more or less irrelevant in a sex object. Ugliness is forgivable in men, but not in women. Consequently and conversely, ugliness is also attributed to any female who might be labeled sinful.

The Grail messenger suffered this fate in myth, because she was of pagan provenance, therefore definable as evil. She became the familiar ugly witch standing by her cauldron. Her sacred vessel of regeneration could be Christianized as a Grail, fictionalized, then dropped and forgotten; but its original earthly counterpart was not so easily erased.

The Crone's cauldron represented the medieval housewife as certainly as an ax represented the woodman, and a bow the hunter. The cauldron was essential for cooking, brewing, processing many kinds of food and medicines, treating hides, washing, dyeing, making household items like soap and candles, carrying fire or water. It was one of the most useful articles in the kitchen. Nothing could have been more appropriate as an emblem of the woman of the house.

Unlike the altars or images of pagan temples, so useful an object as a cauldron could hardly be forbidden and removed from view. Cauldrons were always there. Thus, secret ceremonies involving the cauldron could go on, which is why the cauldron figured in popular ideas about witches.

The Cauldron/Grail, with its inexhaustible capacity for feeding and supporting life, represented not only fertile Mother Earth, but also the essential caring behavior of the female sex, without which any mammalian race would perish. Patriarchal society tends to conceal this basic idea: the human race could probably get along well enough, as it did for many thousands of years, without the chief concerns of its male half, namely competition, warfare, accumulation of personal wealth, and ever-higher technology for its own sake. But the human race could not get along for even one generation if women stopped providing the support system for it all.

The real threat posed by older women in a patriarchal society may be the "evil eye" of sharp judgment honed by disillusioning experience, which pierces male myths and scrutinizes male motives in the hard, unflattering light of critical appraisal. It may be that the witch's evil eye was only an eye from which the scales had fallen.

It was the medieval metamorphosis of the wisewoman into the witch that not only transformed her cauldron from a sacred symbol of regeneration into a vessel of poisons, and changed the word *Crone* from a compliment to an insult, but also established the stereotype of malevolent old womanhood that still haunts elder women today. If a man is old, ugly, and wise, he is a sage. If a woman is old, ugly, and wise, she is a *saga*—that is, a witch.

6

The Crone Turns Witch

Nearly everyone now knows the ugly story of Western man's slaughter of the mothers and grandmothers of his race: the so-called witch mania. Its gruesome details have been described often. Even church-sponsored histories have damningly documented the tortures, the burnings, the seizures of property, the shamelessly rigged trials, the extortion and ecclesiastical flummery that contributed to Europe's five-century craze for gynocide.

Chroniclers spoke of villages where only one or two women were left alive after the inquisitors had done their work.[1] Witch burnings in batches of hundreds, even thousands, were not unknown.[2] At times, what was described as a small forest of stakes was set up for burning masses of people alive. Eighty to ninety percent of the victims were women. All were innocent of the one crime they were convicted for: conspiring with a real devil to destroy God's kingdom by black magic.

Yet, few historians have seriously addressed the really burning question. Why did Western man, with the sanction and encouragement of "his" God, turn on the female of his species and rend her with such savage hatred?

If the answer can be found anywhere, the search must begin with history.

The Inquisition was founded in the twelfth century for the express purpose of exterminating those who held the wrong ideas about religion, that is to say, heretics. Such people dared to criticize the established church for being inhuman, or greedy, or corrupt—all of which it was, at the time. Or, they dared to discuss philosophical and religious doctrines that differed from the party line, at a time when laymen were forbidden to discuss or even think about theology, and were executed as criminals if they were caught reading a Bible in their own language.[3]

The Inquisition carried on the twenty-year mopping-up operation after the Albigensian Crusade in southern France, which wiped out the Provençal population of Catharan dissenters. The Inquisition successfully destroyed large numbers of Jews,

Paulicians, Bogomils, Waldenses, Dolcinists, Fraticelli, Knights Templar, Spiritual Franciscans, Poor Men of Lyons, and other groups accused of antiecclesiastical opinions.

The Inquisition's usefulness was proven beyond a doubt, by the fact that it was enormously profitable, thanks to the rule that every heretic's property could be confiscated immediately, even before trial. There was no need to wait. Torture made conviction virtually a foregone conclusion.[4] People could be tried and convicted even long after they were dead and buried. The property of a deceased heretic's heirs could be seized, to the third generation. The heirs had no choice but to surrender whatever was demanded, or else face the suspicion that might lead them, too, to the torture chamber and stake. No one knew when he might be deprived of all his worldly goods because a long-dead grandparent was suddenly declared a heretic.

When the immediate supply of heretics began to run out, with consequent thinning of profits, the church's elite international terrorist organization had to seek new sources of income. In 1375 a French inquisitor complained that there were no more wealthy heretics left, and "it is a pity that so salutary an institution as ours should be so uncertain of its future."[5] Soon, however, the Inquisition obtained a new lease on life by creating a new form of heresy. To the medieval mind, this was the worst possible kind, because it centered on women—always suspected of a less than total commitment to the patriarchal God who had declared them accursed.

It was said that women should not pray to God for things they really needed, presumably because he wouldn't listen to them. Instead, they should pray to their own ancient Goddess, the Moon Mother.[6] The women who were called "fairies" in medieval Brittany carried on a worship of this Mother in her sacred groves, and were sometimes described as "moon goddesses" (*mandevent*) themselves. Other groups of women who preserved the Old Religion were called Korrigen; they dwelt on islands off the coast, especially the "sacred isle" now called Sein, or Isle of the Saints. They were described as white-haired elder priestesses who danced in groups of nine around their holy fountains by the light of the full moon, wearing robes of white wool. They were once "great princesses"; they hated Christianity because God had cursed them and his priests had driven them into exile.[7]

In the fourteenth century there were still many women practicing at least portions of the religion of their pagan ancestors. Though no longer allowed to be official priestesses of their Goddess as in pre-Christian times, women carried on the "rites of the people" still considered necessary by many to keep natural cycles in working order.[8] Few minds are more conservative than that of the peasant. Six centuries of nominal Christianity failed to eliminate pagan seasonal observances and rituals that the peasants were used to and fond of. Many such rituals still persist to this day, in the customs of Christmas, Easter, May Day, Midsummer, All Hallows, and many saints' days.

Not only the customs of paganism, but also some of the ancient attitudes, persisted among the common people. Among these attitudes was deference toward female tribal elders, which Tacitus mentioned long ago as an outstanding characteristic of the northern barbarians, who based all important decisions on the wisdom of their matriarchs. Despite Christian missionaries' hostility toward tribal matriarchs, deified ancestresses, temple women, and the Mother Goddess who embodied them all, the Christianized barbarians never wholly abandoned their conviction that the real powers controlling their environment and their souls were female powers.

After all, the new faith could hardly alter the fact that all people are born of and guided toward maturity by their mothers. The female archetype was ineradicable for this reason if no other. It was inevitable that Christian missionaries should complain that the native peoples of Europe cared nothing for fatherhood, and regarded the mother's brother as the only important male relative, because he was related by mother-blood.[9]

In addition to their system of matrilineal relationship, European pagans were used to seeking help from the female elders for social, psychological, or physical problems. Medicine was almost exclusively in the hands of old women for countless thousands of years, because of their supposedly innate communion with the Goddess of life and death, until churchmen began to claim that disease could be cured only by holy water, exorcisms, and prayers to God, and by the laying on of priestly hands.[10] During the Middle Ages,

Christianity provided men's primary rationale for taking the practice of healing away from women and converting it into a lucrative male-dominated profession.

Nevertheless, for many centuries the rural areas remained largely free of the officious, interfering, commercial doctors with their leeches and lancets, which usually did more harm than good. Defying the disapproval of parish priests, people continued to take their illnesses and injuries to the village wisewomen, many of whom possessed time-tested knowledge of soothing herbs, anti-inflammatory and antipyretic drugs, practical dentistry and surgery, bonesetting, purging, hypnosis, massage, and other techniques for easing human pains, handed down from prehistoric times by the sacred sisterhoods of the *med-wyf* (wisewomen). "Sorcerers" like Paracelsus and Agrippa von Nettesheim said they learned everything they knew about medicine from such witches.[11] Sometimes, condemned witches were secretly set free by rustic jailers, who thought their healing methods more effective and beneficent than those of their priestly persecutors.[12]

The old *med-wyf* was especially important in matters pertaining to women's mysteries, sexuality and reproduction, which men—even male doctors—usually avoided out of age-old superstitious fear. The *med-wyf* became the "midwife," of whom the inquisitors officially declared, "No one does more harm to the Catholic Faith than midwives."[13]

It was claimed that a midwife harmed the faith by easing women's pain in birth giving, against the will of God who imposed it on women as punishment for Eve's original sin. Not only midwives were burned for witchcraft when accused of engineering a birth without pain, but even women who appealed to them for help in a difficult labor could be condemned also.[14]

It was further claimed that the old wisewomen harmed the faith by helping other women resist male control of their bodies and reproductive functions. Men believed that the midwives knew secret methods of contraception and abortion: forbidden knowledge, in a society where women were supposed to be kept continuously pregnant. Some such information may have been passed down in the matrilineal clans from pre-Christian times. It was an accepted part of the lore of ancient Roman midwife-priestesses, such as the *obstetrix* and *ceraria,* elders in the holy sisterhood of the

Goddess's temples. The witch's broomstick descended from their symbol, a special broom for sweeping a threshold after a birth in the house, to expel evil spirits.[15] In the sixteenth century, Scottish churchwardens were ordered to report to the authorities any such obstetrical "charms, sorcery, enchantments, invocations," and other such "witchcrafts" as the classical priestesses used.[16]

By the fourteenth century, the church had declared war on female healers, stating that if any woman cured sickness without having studied medicine at a university, she was a witch, and must die.[17] The catch was that women were not admitted to universities, which were largely controlled by the church and patronized only by men. Therefore, any female practitioner was without a degree. In 1322, one Jacoba Felicie was arrested and prosecuted for practicing medicine in Paris, though it was recorded that "she was wiser in the art of surgery and medicine than the greatest master or doctor in Paris."[18]

Restrictions on medical training didn't apply to men. Even without a formal education, male wizards or "conjurers" were allowed to cure sickness by magic arts, at the same time when female witches were executed for it.[19]

Sometimes the fatal charge of witchcraft was used to bilk female healers of their fees. A famous witchdoctor, Alison Peirsoun of Byrehill, once cured the archbishop of Saint Andrews of a serious illness. After his recovery, she asked him for payment. He had her arrested and burned for witchcraft.[20]

Laws of the church took away most of women's traditional roles one by one: priestess; midwife; healer; landowner; lawmaker; judge; historian; craftswoman; merchant; record keeper; spiritual advisor; prophet; funerary official; intermediary between heaven, earth, and the underworld. The only female role men could not usurp was that of mother. But even that they tried to take away from women conceptually and symbolically. Fathers of the church proclaimed that the new human soul dwelt only in its father's semen. The mother's body was mere "soil" where the divine seed could grow into a baby. Saint Thomas Aquinas proclaimed this, adding that every girl baby was a defective male, conceived only because her father was ill, weak, or in a state of sin at the time.[21]

However, men of common sense understood that all this was only playing with words; that women really did carry the primary, personal responsibility for the continuing life of the human species. Many men further understood that when they were troubled, sick, hurt, or dying, they wanted the tenderness and sympathy of a woman. They also wanted the practical experience of one who had given birth, fed, nurtured, taught, and nursed others through pains and illnesses: one who had the ancient wisdom.

For such reasons, witchcraft as a profession remained embedded in medieval village life. It was almost the only respectable profession still open to women in the so-called Age of Faith, actually an age of autocratic theocracy. A Dominican father declared that "most women" copied the occult ways of their mother Eve, the first witch; and any woman "by herself" knew more magic than a hundred men.[22] Priests often fumed in irritation while their rivals, the local wisewomen, received honor and payment—to say nothing of gratitude—that the church claimed for God alone.

In such ways the stage was set for the church to develop a new theory of an international heresy, more insidious and far-reaching than any other. This theory advanced the idea that wisewomen were implacable enemies of God, and with the devil's help they were determined to cause as much trouble as possible to pious Christians. If the wisewomen mocked clergymen for their failure to cure, the clergy returned the disparagement a hundredfold, claiming their female rivals invoked the power of demons.

From the ecclesiastical point of view, this was true. Many of the spoken charms and incantations inherited by wisewomen from their predecessors invoked the ancient names of the Goddess and other pagan deities, all of whom had been declared "devils" by the church fathers. Therefore, a charm of protection featuring the once-holy names of Venus and Minerva, instead of "Father, Son, and Holy Ghost," could be technically described as worship of the devil.[23]

Whenever a witch's cure failed and the patient got sicker or died, clergymen were quick to point out that this was God's punishment for consorting with devils. In time, people were brought to doubt the once-trusted priestess. Natural dread of her mysterious powers was carefully augmented to a crippling fear, the kind that finds expression in violence.

The church taught men to fear women. Ecclesiastical writings called woman the confusion of man, an insatiable beast, a continuous anxiety, a daily ruin. Her glances "poison and intoxicate the mind"; her company "induceth impudency, corrupteth virginity, confoundeth and consumeth the bodies, the goods, and the very souls of men." According to Scot, Vairus explained that women by nature have "an unbridled force of fury and concupiscence."[24]

Literature of the Inquisition said witchcraft arose from female carnality, and "all wickedness is but little to the wickedness of a woman."[25] Husbands were advised from the pulpit to beat their wives with whips or sticks, "not in rage but out of charity and concern for her soul, so that the beating will redound to your merit." A twelfth-century Decretum said, "It is right that he whom woman led into wrongdoing should have her under his direction so that he may not fail a second time through female levity." Having a wife under her husband's direction usually meant that he could with impunity beat, "sharply scold, bully and terrify" her.[26]

It is quite possible that sometimes wives subjected to this kind of husbandly "charity" and "concern" might go in desperation to the wisewoman for some means of relief: a spell to make him break his arm, perhaps; or, even more efficacious, a bit of poison. As a rule the law gave her no hope for divorce or separation, and certainly no redress against her assailant. A truly despairing wife would have no way out of the trap, except to kill him or herself. Witches knew how it was. They, too, had fathers and husbands.

The righteous man, given to terrifying women, could always threaten to denounce his wife, mother-in-law, or neighbor to the Inquisition for witchcraft. This was indeed terrifying. Any man's spouse, mother, daughter, or sister could be accused of witchcraft at any time. The accusation could always be made to stick, thanks to the use of torture to obtain confessions.

Churchmen pounded home the message that Satan was busy working his anti-God rebellion through nearly every woman on earth. Being "weaker," a woman was said to be more susceptible to the blandishments of the Evil One than a man. The contradiction inherent in this assertion was somehow never noticed: If man was strong enough to resist the mighty power of Satan, how was it that he couldn't resist the weaker vessel, woman?

Another contradiction lay in the authorities' interpretation of women's motives for practicing witchcraft. The devil was said to reward his servants with earthly wealth and power, yet witches seemed to remain nearly always poor.[27] The charge of witchcraft was to prove a convenient way to get rid of poor widows and other indigent women, too ill or enfeebled to do productive work, therefore a drain on parish funds. When such women became senile or otherwise dependent, they could be called witches and destroyed, like domestic animals past their usefulness.[28]

Male doctors and veterinarians (farriers) found the witchcraft mania very convenient. On the frequent occasions when they failed to cure their patients, they had only to say the cause of the disease was witchcraft. A witch would soon be found to take the blame. The sixteenth-century physician Johann Weyer said priests, too, who "claim to understand the healing art," but do not, simply blamed the nearest witch for any condition they couldn't treat.[29]

Witches became universal scapegoats. When anything went wrong, the weather turned bad, crops failed, houses burned, wagons broke, lightning struck, cows or wells went dry, the cry of witchcraft was raised. When children became disturbed or hysterical, it was demonic possession caused by a witch. All the common troubles of the human condition were attributed to witches during the persecution centuries.

The martyrdom of Jesus as a scapegoat for human sins, of which so much was made, was actually insignificant by comparison with the colossal sum of agony suffered by millions of martyred witches who, though innocent, were forced to assume responsibility for a vast smorgasbord of catastrophes, great and small.

The witch-hunting mania gave men an excuse for their own faults and failures. It was convenient for getting rid of unwanted, poor, solitary, or nonfertile females; contentious wives; rebellious daughters; shrewish neighbors. It made money for the churches. It allowed sexually starved men to sublimate their repressions in the form of sadism. The witch killers were sadists without limit. There was no point where they would voluntarily stop torturing. Records show that the agony could go on for days, weeks, or months, long past the time when victims were wholly broken down, desperate to confess, and pleading to be told what to say, so they could say it.[30]

Inquisitors complacently asserted that in punishment of witches, "eternal damnation should begin in this life, that it might be in some way shown what will be suffered in hell."³¹ Indeed, the vision of hell was invented by men who needed to contemplate victims who could never die, torture that would never end. It was their idea of a suitable reward for their own righteousness. Saint Thomas Aquinas, Saint Bernardino of Siena, and other theologians wrote that not only will "most" of humanity go to hell, but the second greatest pleasure of the blessed ones in heaven—after the pleasure of contemplating God—will be eternally watching the tortures of the damned.³²

Over all, the Age of Faith was a degraded period when the most hideous inhumanity was taken for granted, even viewed as public entertainment; and men routinely inflicted rape, battery, and other physical abuse on women. This was so routine that the symbol of "marriage" in certain holiday decorations was a toy man beating his toy wife.³³ The official religion did not simply permit such abuses, it advocated them as pious duties, meanwhile setting up its own machinery for the inquisitorial system that a respected historian calls unspeakably atrocious, "the most iniquitous that the arbitrary cruelty of man has ever devised."³⁴ The generic "man" is accurate. No women perpetrated this system, except as its victims.

Few men have tried to understand the real causes of man's inhumanity to woman. Among these causes is man's own sense of inferiority in relation to the female archetype of power, which he draws from his infantile experience of total dependence on his mother. Adult men, who might know better if they were thinking rationally, often try to blame women for anything or everything that goes wrong in their lives, as a child might blame his mother for her failure to anticipate every need. Many wives, raised in a patriarchal society that perpetuates the myth of male strength and stoicism, have been disappointed by the fundamental childishness of husbands who expect the wife/mother to somehow "make it all right" and blame her when she can't.³⁵ And few female actions arouse so much male bitterness as what the child typically fears his mother might do: simply walk out, and refuse to return to him. This fear is the root of innumerable patriarchal laws and customs designed to restrict women's freedom. Their religion did not allow medieval men to think of the simple solution to this problem: namely, studying how to please their women, as the ancient

Egyptians did, so they would want to stay close and would enjoy being wives. Instead, men were taught to think of their women as personal slaves.

It was customary to accuse of witchcraft any women living free of male control: self-supporting single women, or widows. There are records of widows so determined to escape another stretch in the prison of marriage, as they saw it, that they fought off amorous suitors as firmly as they could.[36] Men also persecuted women of any unusual skill, knowledge, of physical ability that might make them independent. On one occasion at Newbury, a woman was murdered out of hand by a group of soldiers, because they happened to see her skillfully riding a board on the river, and they instantly decided she must be a witch. When she came ashore, she was seized, slashed, and shot, and her corpse was left where it lay.[37]

The motive of sexual jealousy cannot be omitted from discussion of men's attacks on women. As a general rule, men of intensely patriarchal cultures are poor lovers because they are not taught to pay attention to their partners' needs or feelings. Often, a pretense of hypersexuality is used to conceal what such men know about themselves: that women do not enjoy their attentions. Such secret self-doubt may surface as pathological jealousy.

Literature of the witchcraft period gives the impression that men constantly suspected their wives or mistresses of infidelity. They seemed to believe that every woman was always in search of an adequate lover. Jealous even of women's propensity to stroke and cuddle pet animals, to care for barnyard babies, or to tell their troubles to beasts and birds, men readily believed the churchmen's claims that demon lovers came to women in animal form and turned themselves into handsome men when alone with their mistresses.

Jealousy and secret feelings of sexual inferiority show through the many stories of the demon lover's better lovemaking. It was said demons could please women so much more than mortal men, that the women would find their husbands "paltry and unable to arouse them."[38] In their ignorance of sexual matters, men could think of only one explanation for the demons' superior performance: a penis of "extraordinary largeness." One witch, whose testimony was much quoted and believed, was induced by torture to declare that her demon lover had a member as long and thick as an arm.[39]

Remnants of the bad old days of witchcraft trials are still with us in some ways. Many men are still unaccountably persuaded that penis size is the crucial factor in successful lovemaking. It is perhaps an easy out for those who don't want to bother learning what women really want.

Men's hidden sexual inferiority complexes fostered woman hatred, which was propped up by tales of women's preference for demon lovers and other rivals, less supernatural, but perhaps more intimidating. Members of the male hierarchy seldom trusted one another, in view of the fact that almost any woman could be the sexual prey of any man of higher rank. Fearful of other men who might have more power, patriarchal males vented their anger and mistrust on women, who were actually only passive slaves to the system that exploited their bodies.

Christianity had given men the best of all reasons for hating women when it laid down its doctrine of Eve's responsibility for death. Ever since the early elucidation of this doctrine, every man who feared the approach of death was taught to blame women for it. Death fear runs deep in the human species, the only animal whose intelligence forces it to recognize death's inevitability. And in human myths, the birth-giving, race-founding Mother, mysteriously empowered to create life, always blended with the dread Crone mysteriously empowered to create death.

This blending of apparently contradictory ideas may be explained psychologically by the fact that death fear and mother dependence coexist naturally in the prerational mind of the infant, who recognizes at some level of awareness that to be abandoned by Mother is to die. It is an instinctive recognition, which causes every baby animal to cling to, follow, and watch its mother, and to bawl for her if she is out of sight. Infant apes clutch their mothers' bodies as if their lives depend on it—because they do.

Even more sensitive human infants soon realize that Mother, as a separate entity, could go away and never return. The helpless child would die. The fear enters into the earliest formative layers of the mind, and emerges in those mirrors of the unconscious, myths and religious symbolism. Hence the destroying Crone, co-existent with the Mother. In all lands it was said that a Mother's death curse was the one absolutely inescapable doom, even for gods. As the Markandeya Purana said, "There is nothing anywhere that can dispel the curse of those that have been cursed by a mother."[40]

The fear of abandonment by the life-giving maternal figure surfaces again in later adulthood, when real mothers show signs of aging and sliding downhill toward death, and the individual man even in his prime can note the signs of his own mortality. In a confused sort of way, men were still trying to kill death by killing someone other than themselves. In antiquity, the victims were sacrificial "saviors." In the European Renaissance, the victims were prototypes of Mother Death herself: the witches.

There have been some primitive peoples who steadfastly refused to believe in the natural necessity of death. They insisted that every death was the result of someone's malevolent magic. In effect, Christian theology repeated the same notion. Churchmen decided in the fifth century that it was heresy to believe death natural, not a result of Eve's sin.[41]

Though the *Book of Enoch* said God created death to punish humanity, still in a typically patriarchal blame-the-victim twist, the responsibility was laid on Eve, not God.[42] Saint Paul had excused even Adam, saying only the woman was "in the transgression" (1 Tim. 2:4). This was the canonical view.

On the other hand, the Gnostic gospels of the early Christian era were more inclined to blame God. The *Gospel of Philip* said death came into the world not because of Eve's sin, but because God separated Adam and Eve, who were formerly united in one androgynous body. If Adam were allowed to rejoin his mate, who gave him life, and "again becomes complete and attains his former self, death will be no more."[43] Obviously the result of Tantric influence, in the tradition of the primal Mother-Father, this notion entered into the medieval Cabala and other occult systems.

The limitless ferocity of the clergy toward witches probably stemmed from the fact that they served a church that claimed to have conquered death, yet they continued to see death all around them, especially in the terrible century of the plague. In the real world, death seemed as unconquerable as ever. Only in the mind's eye could death be held at bay by the intangible promises of faith.

Sometimes these promises were not enough to maintain the vision against the evidence of reality.

If woman could be blamed for the unsettling disparity between the desired vision of immortality and the undesired demonstrations of mortality in organic life, man might kill her in order to kill his own doubts. Medieval Europe tried to amputate that half of the ancient philosophy that made woman responsible for life (allocating this function to God), yet retain that half that made her equally responsible for death. As the fertile sex, women could also be blamed for infertility, in every manifestation from miscarriages to crop failure. "Droughts and catastrophes from bad weather" were also attributed to witches, or women generally.[44] In many ways, indeed, Christianity's universal scapegoat was not Christ but woman.

Since the pagan ruler of death was usually the Crone in the guise of an old woman, and elder priestesses had occupied the honored positions in pagan temples, old women became the most frequent victims of witch persecutions. Women after menopause no longer served the purposes of the patrilineal family system, which viewed women as breeding machines and even made "barrenness" a legal reason for a man to abandon his wife. The earlier ramified functions of the elder woman, as educator, record keeper, healer, arbiter of morality, and so on, had been handed over to the patriarchal church. The same church helped codify laws that deprived elder women of the wealth and property they used to control under the rules of mother-right. Consequently, the old woman was an ideal scapegoat: too expendable to be missed, too weak to fight back, too poor to matter.

Old women could survive in such a society by assuming the lowest possible profile, to be always self-effacing, undemanding, hardworking, and anxious to please. Old women who dared to be cranky, crotchety, or outspoken could even be marched off to prison. If they were too critical or insulting toward men, they could lose their lives for it.

Female "scolding" was defined as a crime during the Renaissance. In Britain this crime was punished by a torture device called the brank, or scold's bridle, which locked the victim's head inside an iron cage that drove spikes through her tongue or cheeks. This device was still in use during the nineteenth century. Alternatively, scolds could be punished with the same ducking stool used to drown, or half-drown, witches, by ducking them under water in stagnant ponds or cesspools.[45]

The crime of scolding may have been named for the Goddess Skuld, mistress of the death curse, Crone aspect of the three Norns (Fates), and fount of witchlike "skulduggery." From the earliest times, men feared women's derogatory words, because they thought women had the numinous power to make their words come true: the same power that eventually assumed a Christianized form under its Greek title of *Logos,* the Power of the Word. This was more than a mere symbol. If a woman cursed a man with death, calling on her Goddess to hear and actualize the curse, the man cursed could so firmly believe in her power that he would, in fact, pine away and die. The curse was thought especially efficacious if the woman was a priestess or a mother. For this reason the biblical Hannah said, when she became a mother, "My mouth is enlarged over mine enemies" (1 Sam. 2:1), meaning that her curses became more formidable.

Christian men, already laboring under a burden of guilt in relations with women, were horrified by any woman who didn't hesitate to damn them out loud. Naturally it was the older, more experienced women who were more likely to speak their minds about their disillusionments or their bitterness. By persecuting them as witches, men sought to deprive them even of the last right of self-expression that powerless men claim for themselves: bitching.

Sometimes, the implied death curse associated with female scolding was interpreted as castration, or death of the "little man" (penis). This simplistic male reaction can be heard today, not only in the Freudian-conventional non sequitur that calls man-criticizing women castraters, but even in the works of professionals, whose thinking should attain a somewhat higher level of organization. As Adrienne Rich says, "A plain fact cleanly spoken by a woman's tongue is not infrequently perceived as a cutting blade directed at a man's genitals."[46] Popes and priests of the Inquisition firmly believed that witches' words could take away men's virility and even their sexual organs without any physical contact at all.[47]

In return for the imagined castration, men sometimes tried to retaliate in kind, symbolically castrating women by denying their sexuality. Thus, women who dared to be defiant were often called ugly—that is, sexually unattractive—even when their appearance was wholly irrelevant to the issue. Therefore the witch became, as a stereotype, both old and ugly.

The ancients did not consider the signs of old age any uglier in women than in men. In some cultures, old age was even thought attractive; young people craved gray hair and wrinkles to show they had grown old enough to command respect. A remnant of such attitudes is seen in the British courts, where officials wear white wigs, originally supposed to suggest the white hair of judicious age.

However, once old women were deprived of wisewoman status, their appearance was denigrated also. It became the conventional opinion that all old women were ugly, and witches were the ugliest of old women. Reginald Scot described witches as old, lame, bleary eyed, pale, foul, wrinkled, poor, sullen, lean, deformed, melancholic, mad, superstitious scolds. Yet he was a sixteenth-century skeptic who did not believe witches had magic power. He scoffed at the notion that women would make pacts with the devil, since any woman of common sense could see that the devil's promise to protect his witch from arrest and execution was entirely worthless. The devil's bargain brought the witch nothing, neither "beauty, money, promotion, wealth, worship, pleasure, honor, knowledge, learning, or any other benefit whatsoever."[48]

Sometimes it was claimed that ugly old witches, being shapeshifters, could make themselves young and beautiful when they chose, in addition to turning themselves into cats, crows, hares, or mares. It was said of the mysterious Korrigen sisterhood that they were beautiful women by night, and white-haired, red-eyed, wrinkled crones by day.[49] Perhaps they were aged priestesses who wore masks or makeup for their ceremonies.

Male attitudes toward women's makeup have always been ambivalent. Patriarchal custom denounced women both for looking old and for using makeup to try not to look old. Some religious groups, such as the Quakers, condemned all cosmetics as snares of the devil. Yet, a majority of men learned to perceive women as unfeminine if they refused to use cosmetics. On the other hand, in 1770 the British Parliament levied the same penalties as for witchcraft upon any woman who enticed a man into marriage with such artificial aids as perfume, paints, corsets, false hair, false teeth, or high-heeled shoes.[50]

Our very language demonstrates that men expected women's sexual attractiveness to depend on trickery, or witchery. An alluring woman still "casts a spell"; she is charming, enchanting, bewitching, entrancing, tempting, fascinating; or she is *glamorous*, a word that came from the magic of Morgan-the-Crone, Goddess of Glamorgan.

Woman's sexual magnetism is still experienced by man as a disquieting sort of magic, poorly understood, inflicting a sense of helplessness. Probably this has been so ever since men began to fear women's uncanny ability to force embarrassing responses from male genitals, even across a distance, by words or gestures alone.

The witchcraft mania in Western civilization was not so long ago, nor so far away, that its effects have been wholly eradicated in our own time. We may trace to the era of persecution our society's view of old women as ugly or obnoxious, and especially the refusal to recognize the mental capabilities of elder women, to honor their life experience as enlightening, or to realize that they may be better qualified than men to establish standards of morality.

Millions of intelligent, perceptive, talented elder women remain trapped in uninteresting lives because modern society provides no useful channels for their ambition or energy. After producing and raising their children, most women are expected to fade away into the mass of nonproductive consumers, to spend the culmination of their adulthood on childish pastimes like those of teenage girls, including useless worrying about their appearance, so that the cosmetics corporations may grow rich and prosperous.

Over a century ago, in a speech in Philadelphia, a woman physician called for "the right, scarcely yet conceded to women, to grow old without reproach."[51] The right has not yet been conceded. In the fantasyland men create to sell products, via television and other media, "the woman over thirty has been annihilated."[52] Though the products for sale include many aimed directly at the aging woman, such as cosmetics to make her look more sexy (that is, younger), "women are permitted to be sexual only at a certain time of life, and the sensuality of mature—and certainly of aging

—women has been perceived as grotesque, threatening, and inappropriate."[53]

It is instructive to analyze what men define as appropriate for a woman to do or be. Postmenopausal sexuality would naturally be seen as inappropriate in a society that viewed women as baby-making machines. Only a few centuries ago in history, male arbiters of morality in our culture insisted that the sexuality of older women was not only inappropriate, but an indication of profound evil, inspired by the devil himself.

In such a society it would hardly be surprising to find numbers of women subject to various neurotic fancies and complaints triggered by simple sexual frustrations. Studying so-called witches' descriptions of their demon lovers' attentions, Weyer described them as mere fantasies arising from women's "melancholic" dreams. Clergymen denounced this rationalistic view, for Weyer was "talking like a rational human being to the inmates of a gigantic insane asylum." All the way up to the early twentieth century, depressions in middle-aged women were called "mildly immoral." A doctor scorned such women for going into "a chronic state of martyrdom" and claiming their husbands didn't understand them. It seemed not to enter the doctors' heads that husbands did not, in fact, understand or even tolerate their wives very well, and the women's sense of martyrdom was often quite firmly founded in reality.[54]

One of the cruelest aspects of the witchcraft persecution was its punishment of women for doing things that men were free to do, such as practicing medicine, reading philosophy, training animals, giving spiritual advice, studying the lore of nature, alchemy, or the stars. Out of these and many similar sexist prohibitions arose the myths of women's mental limitations, to haunt and hamper bright, curious-minded women in our own time.

Men have consistently tried to prevent women from studying certain subjects, by the argument that women can't understand the subject matter. Of course, if they really couldn't understand it, there would be no need for the prohibition. Here again, it was a matter of barring the path for all women with the conventional rubric "Inappropriate." Women who showed themselves quite capable of grasping the principles and practice of medicine, mathematics, mechanics, law, or any other male-dominated field, were called unfeminine by reason of excessive intelligence. Stupidity, therefore, was to be defined as a typically feminine quality. So the vicious circle continued.

Even necromancy, that traditional sin of witches, for which the biblical witches were killed (Exodus 22:18, 1 Sam. 28:9), was permissible for male practitioners only. One of the early popes practiced necromancy with the aid of a wizard, to learn about life after death.[55] Reginald Scot wondered why it was a legitimate miracle for Christ to call up the dead, but a crime for a witch to do likewise.[56] In 1675, the results of clergymen's necromantic pursuits were published by the monk Albert de Saint Jacques, in a book entitled *Light to the Living by the Experiences of the Dead,* purporting to explain the afterworld by quotations from the mouths of those who dwelt in it.[57] If the author had been a woman, she would have been killed.

What men learned from women, however, women could relearn from men. The practice of necromancy continued in female hands, where it is often found today, under the new name of spiritualism. One may suspect that ecclesiastical authorities denounce spiritualism for the primary reason that most "spirit mediums" are female, rather than for the more pragmatic reason that most of them are conscious frauds. Ecclesiastical authorities themselves are often conscious unbelievers, but they support one another in claiming all manner of access to the supernatural for their own fraternity alone.

This, indeed, was the real issue of the witchcraft mania: the churches' denial of spiritual authority to women on any level, from the primitive kind of credulity that bought and sold blessed medals, holy water, fake relics, and indulgences, as well as witch charms, to the most esoteric circular reasoning that gave rise to the pseudoscience of theology. During the fourteenth century, certain orders of teaching nuns were proscribed because the sisters had committed the "mad" offense of daring to discuss theological matters among themselves.[58]

The Inquisition's campaign to cut women off from their own direct experience of spiritual vision, or their Goddess-given moral codes, occupied nearly five centuries of European history. About nine million persons were executed after 1484, and uncounted numbers before that date, mostly women. The executions were carried out with a febrile brutality exceeding that of any other organized persecution ever known, not excepting the Nazis' twentieth-century holocaust, even though some modern historians have tried to declare the latter without precedent.[59]

Persecutions are fueled by man's favorite We/They myth, which presents one's own group as the epitome of virtuous humanity, and any different group as somehow subhuman, sinful, deserving extermination. Long centuries of discriminatory customs and propaganda had prepared the good Christian patriots of twentieth-century Germany to accept the idea that their troubles were caused by non-Teutonic *Untermenschen* (subhumans) in their midst, and to accept, also, Hitler's "final solution" of organized massacre. Similarly, nineteenth-century Americans accepted the idea that blacks deserved to be enslaved, and Indians deserved to be robbed of their lands and killed off, because they were not-quite-human savages. The fact that these kinds of persecution were immensely profitable to the persecutors was rarely mentioned. It was the same in the case of the Inquisition, which actually killed for money and greatly enriched the church with its rules of confiscation.[60]

Through *all* the centuries, however, male-centered Western civilization viewed women as "the other," hence ideal universal scapegoats for all mishaps, including the inevitable mishap of death. Male spiritual authorities constantly supported this view. Women became the scapegoats for men's fear of the punishing Father, whom they created out of their own nightmarish visions. Thus, religious leaders encouraged sadistic attacks on the womenfolk of their communities: especially the maternal elders, who used to command respect as rival religious leaders. Before persecution of witches caught on in Scotland, the popular Scottish term for a witch was "friend of man."[61]

It would be a strange revolution indeed if women as a group ever became as cold, brutal, and arrogant toward the male sex as the male sex has been toward women in historical times. Somehow, women managed to forgive, and forgive, and forgive again, excusing male misbehavior on the ground that men were like little boys and could not be expected to assume truly mature responsibility for their actions. However, accused witches, while screaming on the rack, probably did not think so kindly of their torturers as mere grown-up little boys who didn't know any better.

Like any other oppressed or enslaved group, women often sought self-protection in elaborate charades of harmlessness, designed to reassure the oppressor that no offense was meant. When old women were declared enemies of God and "man," old women tended to walk carefully, speak quietly, hide their bodies in funereal clothes, keep their eyes downcast. From such habits of protective coloration arose today's stereotype of the sweet little old lady, or the granny next door, the acceptable old woman who makes no judgments and speaks only to bubble cheery platitudes. The shrewdly critical, thinking, challenging sort of old woman might be condescendingly termed "feisty," but some men still show as much suspicion of her as centuries ago, when she could be legally mutilated and burned as a witch.

The real solution to this problem is not to assume the protective coloring of sweet-little-old-ladyism in the hope of escaping notice. Not being sadistic as a rule, women often fail to understand the basic fact about sadistic behavior: It is not allayed but stimulated by the appearance of vulnerability in the prospective victim. It would be better for old women to assert their right to judge, to be bolder in questioning male authority, to demand the respect due them as mothers and as decent, caring citizens. Younger women should also uphold the ideals of feminine authority, so their own later cronehood will not be blighted by fear or contempt.

When, by a heavy statistical preponderance of over ninety percent, men are the real killers in human society, the malevolent old witch is hardly a valid image of aging womanhood, even if she is confused with the archetypal Crone. The witch was a victim, not an aggressor. The Crone, never victimized really, can still serve women as an empowering image of biological truth, female wisdom, and mother-right, to which men must learn to defer, if they are ever to conquer the enemy within themselves.

7

The Doomsday Crone

7

Centuries before Christianity came to Iceland, a priestess there assembled ancient traditions into a poem, the *Völuspá* or "Priestess's Prophecy," a pagan equivalent of our Book of Revelation. She described Ragnarök, the end of the world, with its usual, universal details: great fires, floods, earthquakes, crumbling mountains, stars falling from heaven, darkening of the sun and moon, the rising of the Great Serpent from the abyss, with terrible battles and cataclysms carrying down to destruction all humanity and all the gods—but not, significantly, the goddesses.

After a timeless time, there would be a new creation. The second coming of Balder, Son of God, would herald a new, improved race of deities. A new earth would rise from the formless Deep (Ginnungagap). Cataracts would fall again from the cliffs. The righteous ones would dwell in a hall brighter than the sun, and the latter would be a new sun, brilliant daughter of the old Sun Goddess who was named Glory-of-Elves.

The human race would be renewed by a couple living on the morning dew, in the magical environment of the World Tree. The woman would be named Life, and the man Desirer-of-Life.[1] As the new Adam and Eve, this pair recalls the original Hittite name of Eve, which was Hawwah, meaning "Life."[2]

In broad outline, this was the same Indo-European doomsday myth known throughout the Eurasian continent. It was a myth of incalculable age, perhaps dating from humanity's earliest recognition that whatever had a beginning must have an end, even the universe itself. The doomsday myth is found in all cultures. Versions appearing in northern Europe show a clear affinity with those of southeastern Asia, revealing their prehistoric kinship.

Scandinavians said the fire god Surt would come with his flaming host from the hot land far to the south, Mutspellheim, the Land of Mother's Curse, to burn up the world. Surt seems to be identical with the Vedic fire god Agni, who was described in the same words. His hot southern land was almost certainly India, home of Crone Mother Kali who was to bring the world to an end with her curse.[3]

There are many other parallels between the myths of India and those of northern Europe. There were the archaic many-armed deities of Scandinavia, such as the god Starkad, whose extra arms had to be removed. There were the Great Mother's magical creative powers, called *siddhi* in the south, *sidh* or *seidr* in the north. There were the primal sages of gigantic stature, southern *rishi*, northern *risi*, and the human sacred kings entitled *raj*, *rex*, *reg*, or *rig*. There was black Kali herself, the Great Shadow or the Formless One, both north and south, swallowing all the gods at the end of the world. At doomsday, Kali would become the Void or Abyss of primordial nonform, the black Crone who, "at the final dissolution," devours everything she brought forth: "As white, yellow, and other colors all disappear in black, in the same way . . . all beings enter Kali."[4]

As the northern Goddess Skadi, she became the Black Shadow that ate all the gods at their *Götterdämmerung* or "Twilight," a rather inaccurate translation of the Going-Into-the-Shadow of the gods. Ginnungagap the Abyss that swallowed all things, and from which all things arose at creation, was a northern version of Kali's dark womb of chaos, formlessness, or voidness.[5] The Celtic version of the same symbol was Mother Sulis, the female gap, or eye, or black hole, or cauldron: the cosmic yoni.

In the Icelandic version, the final Armageddon-like battle of the gods opens with the last trump blown on the "ringing horn" (*Gjallarhorn*) of the god Rig-Heimdall, whose title means "king" and is cognate with Sanskrit *raj*. One of the dire omens announced by his blast is the breaking away of the death ship Naglfar from her moorings. This curious ship is made entirely of dead men's fingernails. The tale of the *Völuspá* pauses to warn that the dead should always have their nails cut short, so the ship's completion will be delayed as long as possible. Apparently there was a belief that when the nails of the dead had finally provided enough material to finish the ship Naglfar, doomsday would be imminent. The superstitious custom of trimming corpses' fingernails persists to this day.

The Prose Edda gives four variations on the theme of God's engulfment, when the sky-father disappears into the gaping maw of the death dog, variously called the Great Wolf of the North, Fenrir, Managarm, Hàti, or Skoll. The sun and moon are swallowed by the latter two, though in the darkness the Sun Goddess Glory-of-Elves will bring forth her daughter to illuminate the next new creation: a future female *Fiat lux*. The giant wolves devour the gods Odin and Tyr, who are later and earlier versions, respectively, of the original Indo-European sky father.[6] His Eastern name has been rendered Dyaus, Daevus, or Djevs; sometimes Ieu or Jeu. He is identical with the Greeks' Zeus and the Roman Deus, meaning simply "God."

The story of God's engulfment by the Wolf of the North had interesting interpretations in Slavic and Balkan cultures, including the traditions of early Greece. The Slavs' Triple Goddess of Fate, the three Zorya, kept this mighty canine fastened by an iron chain to the hub of the heavens, the north celestial pole, marked by the star Polaris in the constellation of Ursa Minor. It was said that the end of the world would arrive when the wolf-dog was released from his chain.[7] The Greek sect of Cynics, founded by the famous sage Diogenes, had still another version of the same myth that sheds considerable light on the rationale of the doomsday story everywhere.

The Cynics considered themselves the Great Mother's "watchdogs." Their name came from *kynikos*, "doglike ones." They carefully watched the north star, Polaris, which they called *kynos oura*, "the Dog's Tail"; they saw the constellation Ursa Minor as a dog or wolf. Since it was (and is) the still point of the turning heavens, the Dog's Tail became the "cynosure" or focus of attention.[8] The Cynics said the end of the world would be at hand when they saw this star begin to move from its fixed place in the middle of the heavens.

Diogenes, founder of the sect of Cynics, renounced all worldly considerations and lived an ascetic life, like an Eastern yogi. He denounced the rich for their self-indulgent habits. He urged repentance and a return to simplicity. He made his home in a great earthenware tub (or cauldron) beside the Great Mother's temple, declaring that no one needed any more spacious accommodation than that. The story goes that he searched with a lighted lantern, even during the day, for one honest man. This was no mere eccentricity. It had a symbolic meaning.

Like certain Christian sects after them the Cynics firmly believed the wickedness and loose living of humans were going to bring doomsday down on the world. Apparently they claimed the Great Mother would not launch her doomsday curse as long as there remained in the world one honest man to preserve the right values.

No one said whether Diogenes found his honest man or not. However, he had small respect for the world's rich and mighty. An apocryphal story said Diogenes was much admired by Alexander the Great, who went to visit the sage in his tub and offered to do anything Diogenes wanted. Sitting under the king's shadow, Diogenes made only one request: that Alexander should stand out of his light.

The honest-man myth is significant. Everywhere, the idea of doomsday was bound up with the idea that humanity was falling into sinfulness and crime. This would bring on the ultimate wrath of the destroying Crone, whose anger would devour the world.

According to the Icelandic prophetess, the beginning of the end would find all men embroiled in war, butchery, and sordid greed. Brothers would slay each other and incestuously rape their sisters. Family members would have no respect for parenthood or blood bonds. Tribes and nations would be at war, even against kinfolk. This terrible time, called the Age of the Wolf, would be followed by the Monstrous Winter when the world would have no more summertime for three years in a row.[9] Modern scientists have postulated the same idea, calling it the "nuclear winter."

The theme of a sinful betrayal of ancient standards was equally prominent in Celtic legends of the coming Waste Land, which was also a kind of apocalypse brought on by human faults. According to the Irish Fate Goddess Babd, the "Boiling One" of the cauldron, the Waste Land would come upon the world when "old men would give false judgments and legislators make unjust laws; warriors would betray one another, and men would be thieves, and there would be no more virtue left in the world."[10]

Scandinavian, Greek, and Celtic prophecies might be traced back to the fountainhead of Indo-European thought, the religion of Mother Kali, probably the original doomsday Crone. Kali's worshipers believed there must be four ages of the world, called *yugas,* comparable to the Greeks' gold, silver, bronze, and iron ages. In each *yuga,* people became progressively less peaceful and happy as more millenia separated them from the Mother-dominated time, the childhood of the cosmos: a concept undoubtedly derived from memories of real childhood manipulated by the collective unconscious.

Kali's sages said the first of the four world ages was the best, because all life was "centered in the blood"—that is, in an abundance of the Goddess's world-creating menstrual fluid, the medium of the transmission of life, which made the earth very fertile, and its people wise, sinless, peaceable, and long lived. People grew to the stature of giants, lived a thousand years, and died only when they wished to.[11]

Similar Scandinavian myths placed the race of giants in an earlier age of the world, though the god Thor was able to travel to their hidden country to seek the ancient wisdom, by swimming a river filled with the menstrual blood of the giantesses.[12] The same river of blood appeared in Celtic myth around the borders of the Fairy Queen's paradise. Certain Goddess-loving heroes, such as Thomas Rhymer (Thomas of Erceldoune), were allowed to swim or wade across and spend a certain time—usually seven years—in this magic land. The fairies may have been ancestral giants before they became "little people," diminished by centuries of belittling. Their queen was often called Titania, meaning the mother of the Titans, a Greek term for the gigantic primordial children of the Goddess Earth.

Influenced by the same myth cycle, writers of the Bible claimed "there were giants in the earth" shortly after the creation (Gen. 6:4), and the early patriarchs lived to great ages, close to the Hindus' canonical thousand years. The Bible asserts that Adam lived nearly a thousand years (Gen. 5:5), and Philo maintained that Adam was a giant. Abraham, too, was said to have been seventy times the size of a normal man.[13] There are still people among the Arabs who believe local megalithic structures were built by antediluvian giants.[14]

Of course there is nothing so strange about making giants of the deified or semideified ancestors. Consciously or not, we all remember a time when we lived in a world peopled by giants, or at least by individuals much larger than ourselves. As adults we tend to forget this central fact of childhood existence; but the mythmaking faculty, the collective unconscious, does not.

Hindus said that with the passing of the ages, people shrank in stature, longevity, intelligence, and moral fiber, until the present *yuga* finds them reduced to small minds and bodies that cannot last even a century. No longer "centered in the blood," human society has lost its ancient virtues. In this age, wealth is the only standard of worth, property confers rank, lying brings worldly success, sexual passion is the only enjoyment and the only connection between spouses, and "outer trappings are confused with inner religion."[15] Because of their "lust and limited intelligence," men of this age are unable to recognize the divine spirit in women, where the Holy Shakti manifests herself.[16]

This present age is called the Kali Yuga, because Kali the Destroyer will bring it to an end, out of disgust for its sin and violence. The signs of oncoming doom appear: "Old people, destitute of the true wisdom of old age, try to behave like the young, and the young lack the candor of youth. . . . The bonds of sympathy and love have dissolved; narrow egotism rules."[17]

As in the West, the texts suggest that this literature grew out of a period of transition from Goddess worship and mother-centered kinship systems, to the patriarchal gods and patrilineal clans characteristic of later Aryan cultures. The last days are said to come about because men don't respect the wisdom of their mothers and wives; because they become greedy and exploitive; and because they follow warlike gods, who preach violence and conquest. They have forgotten love and caring; they evade responsibility; they have no honor. Therefore the angry Mother curses such men and their gods into destruction, whether she is called Kali, Skadi, Nemesis, Erinys, Hecate, Macha, Anath, Cerridwen, Hel, Morgan, or a dozen other Death Goddess names. Whatever her name, she became the Mother about to use her dread maternal power to devour the gods she brought forth. Since a Mother's curse is irresistible, as her curse echoes from "Mutspellheim," the gods themselves go mad in the final paroxysms of the universe.

In view of the world situation today, it must be granted that there is a curiously disturbing pertinence to these ancient doom-sayings. One might think that, in their times of ideological change, the priestesses foresaw that the triumph of patriarchal religion and male dominance would threaten the peace of their tribes, destroy their sense of mutual responsibility, and set up a hierarchy of militaristic aggression. Perhaps the wisewomen intuitively understood what would happen when male value systems overrode female ones. They must have foreseen that a patriarchal society would maintain itself by balances of conflict and armed truce rather than by altruism, and by runaway exploitation rather than by care for nature's resources.

So deeply embedded was the doomsday myth in the ancient world that it could not be ignored or forgotten by patriarchal sects. It even had an archetypal validity that made it psychologically necessary to many men, as will be shown. Therefore, patriarchal thinkers were obliged to adapt it to their new value system by means of new interpretations. They could hardly allow destruction of the matrilineal clan to be called the cause of the world's end, since destruction of the matrilineal clan was what they wanted. Early patriarchal thinkers may have been genuinely frightened by the Crone's death curse, and earnestly desirous of seeking a way around it.

Perhaps the first to evolve an acceptable new view of doomsday were the Persians, whose prophet Zoroaster said the only women worthy of paradise were those "submissive to control, who had considered their husbands lords."[18] For his followers, there was no Mother-dominated cyclic universe. The cyclic became linear. There was only one creation, only one doomsday. Afterward, any existence on the material plane would cease. For the individual or the cosmos, life was a straight line from beginning to end. There would be no return, rebirth, regeneration, or renewal, no turning of the karmic wheel toward new beginnings. Later Christians based their rejection of the ancient worldwide doctrine of reincarnation on these Persian precedents, saying God appointed death for men only once, and after this would come the judgment (Heb. 9:27).

At this point the cross could replace the cauldron as a cosmic symbol. Worshipers of Mithra and Zoroaster marked their communion cakes with the sign of the cross.[19] From the beginning this was a masculine sign, originally representing a phallus. It also stood for all kinds of divisions, separations, quarterings. Unlike the feminine symbol of the circle, the cross had upper and lower, right and left parts. It was hierarchical and categorical, classifying rather than including. Patriarchal societies tended to build square towns, oriented by the cross to what men decided must be four cardinal directions. Matriarchal villages were round.

For a while, cross and circle symbolically coexisted, as in the cauldron and lance, the Egyptian ankh, the cross of Wotan, the mirror of Venus, and the Celtic cross—actually a Hindu glyph of male and female powers in conjunction. Now, even these cross-and-loop or cross-and-circle designs are known as types of crosses. The circular portion of the design is ignored as meaningless. Early in the Christian era, many such designs were deprived of their female components.

The Persians similarly amputated the female part of their primal androgynous world creator, Zurvan or "Infinite Time," the same name applied to Kali-the-Crone. Though Zurvan was usually called masculine, the Persians incongruously insisted that God and the devil (Ahura Mazda and Ahriman) were born simultaneously from Zurvan's *womb*. This peculiarly womb-equipped First Cause also bore the names of Time, Destiny, and Fate: the usual titles of the Triple Goddess.[20]

Zurvan's twin offspring provided the basis for the later tale of Cain and Abel, as well as for many ideas about the opposing principles of good and evil, when Ahura Mazda made the right sacrifices and was elevated to the solar kingship of heaven, while Ahriman made unacceptable sacrifices and was thrust down to the underworld, where he became the Black Sun or the Great Serpent. Though he was a dark god later assimilated into the composite picture of the devil, the Magi worshiped him, viewing him as the source of their magical wisdom. Like other versions of the Great Serpent, he lived in the womb of the Mother, and understood her secrets.

Ahriman was originally the Hindu god Aryaman, one of the twelve zodiacal sons of the celestial Goddess Aditi, and the father of "Aryan" tribes.[21] In Ireland, he was remembered as the legend-ary King Eremon, whose law was that royal succession was to pass only in the female line: an obvious leftover from earlier ma-triarchy.[22] Possibly the Persians diabolized Ahriman for the very reason that he was closely connected with the Old Religion. Cer-tainly the subterranean Great Serpent was long regarded every-where as the phallic god whose great wisdom stemmed from his intimate contact with Mother Earth's uterine depths. He fertilized the Goddess Jahi, the Persians' counterpart of Eve or Lilith—and perhaps the name Hebrews masculinized into Jah, Jahveh or Yahweh—so she might bring forth the primordial "blood of life" and create a world population. Similarly, it was said that the serpent fertilized Eve.

Unlike European Aryans, the Persians gave no reason for the onset of doomsday. Once they had removed the Goddess from their story, there was no death curse to be pronounced. It wasn't the sin of male violence that brought on the last days. This idea would hardly have served a military dictatorship, engaged in winning its empire by force of arms. The Persians decided that somehow, doomsday would just happen.

To place the solar god higher in their hierarchy than the subterranean Great Serpent, Persian priests began to tell the story of the war in heaven. They said Ahriman was once a heavenly angel, but he rebelled against the authority of his brother god. Armies then formed on both sides, among the *daevas,* a word meaning both "god" and "devil" but sometimes translated "angel."[23] The followers of Ahriman were blamed for all trickery and falsehood, so they became what the Western world was to envision as fallen angels or "devils."

Although the forces of light were supposed to have won the war in heaven for all time, for some unspecified reason there had to be another war between the same two powers at the end of the world. Again the fallen angels under Ahriman would fight the heavenly angels under Ahura Mazda, whose symbol was the sun, and whose title, Light of the World, was inherited by the Christian deity. This final battle became the familiar Armageddon or—as Persian-influenced Jewish Essenes would have it—"the War of the Sons of Light with the Sons of Darkness."[24] The latter were also known as "men of the Pit."[25]

Thus the Persian sages and their Essenic admirers fell into the common error of unnecessary duplication of myths. When the battle between good and evil angels took place before the origin of the earth, the evil ones were supposed to have been utterly vanquished and imprisoned in the underworld for all time. However, it was obvious even to the minimally observant that evil was by no means vanquished. Everyone knew that evil spirits traveled freely throughout the world, causing all sorts of mischief, while the heavenly god did nothing about it. Clearly, he had not really restricted their power at all. If virtue was to triumph at the end of the world, according to the new patriarchal scenario, then another battle was required.

Some day, then, without any particular stimulus, the war would begin again. It was to be accompanied by the usual apocalyptic symptoms: great fires, floods, crumbling mountains, falling stars, all the elements returning to their original formless state.[26] This time, the priests declared, the victory of heaven's forces would be final. A last judgment would pass the human "elect" to their eternal paradise, while the wicked would go to dwell in outer darkness with Ahriman and his devils.

Among these Persian devils was a male spirit of devastation called Aeshma, who may have begun as an archaic form of the destroying Crone. Aesh-Ma could be rendered "Mother of Wisdom" or "Mother of the Holy Law," common epithets for the Crone. Jewish writers of the *Book of Tobit* adopted Aeshma as the lecherous demon Asmo-daeva, or Asmodeus, under which name "he" passed into Christian tradition as one of the horned and fanged celebrities of hell.

Of course the chief celebrity of hell was the fallen angel Lucifer, also known as Satan, Beelzebub, Hades, Pluto, Belial, Leviathan, and several other names of earlier gods identified with Ahriman. Lucifer means "Light Bringer," the Latin name for the god of the morning star, the sun's herald, whom Canaanites called Shaher. An old Canaanite myth concerning this god became confused with the Persians' war in heaven story, and out of this confusion arose the primary Christian concept of an evil deity.

Many people have the erroneous impression that the war in heaven is described in the Bible as having taken place some time before the incident in Eden, since the fallen "serpent" (Lucifer/Satan) was already present in the garden. But this was a Persian tale; no such story appears in the canonical Scriptures.

The only Old Testament mention of a fallen Lucifer is a very late insertion in the book of Isaiah: "How art thou fallen from heaven, O Lucifer, son of the morning! How art thou cut down to the ground, which didst weaken the nations! For thou hast said in thine heart, I will ascend into heaven, I will exalt my throne above the stars of God: I will sit also upon the mount of the congregation, in the sides of the north: I will be like the most High" (Isa. 14:-12–13).

Yet this fragment was no genuine Semitic tradition, but a bit of plagiarism from the Canaanites, who assumed that their morning-star god envied the superior brightness of the sun and tried to seize the solar throne, for which offense he was thrown down from heaven (that is, his light went out with the arrival of the sun). In the seventh century B.C., the Canaanites wrote a dirge for him: "How hast thou fallen from heaven, Helel's son Shaher! Thou didst say in thy heart, I will ascend to heaven, above the circumpolar stars I will raise my throne, and I will dwell on the Mount of Council in the back of the north; I will mount on the back of a cloud, I will be like unto Elyon."[27] This was written long before the Jews adopted the war in heaven myth. Its reappearance in the Bible was intended only as a metaphoric illustration of how "the mighty" could find themselves fallen if they allowed their hubris to go too far. Like everything else in the Bible it was taken much too literally by people who later decided that every word in the canonical books proceeded directly from the mouth of God.

Jewish Essenes adopted the Persian cosmogony, and determined to be among the elect at the world's end, which they expected almost immediately. The Essenes were ascetic desert anchorites who rejected all pleasures of the flesh, like Eastern yogis, in order to purify their souls before the coming judgment.

Each Essenic community included a functionary known as the Christ or Anointed One, "head of the congregation," and another called the Teacher of Righteousness or Messiah of Israel.[28] Messiah (Hebrew *Mashiach*) was a Persian title. So was "Son of Man," used in the Gospels for the doomsday description of "the Son of Man coming in a cloud with power and great glory" (Luke 9:27, 21:27).

Jesus was said to have spent his early years in an Essene community. His period of fasting and meditation alone in the "wilderness" was a typical Essene initiation requirement. His basic message was the Essenic one of oncoming doomsday, which he said would occur within his own generation (Luke 9:27). Of course he was wrong; but early Christians continued to look for the world's end at any moment, as did the Essenes. The two sects were not always distinguishable. The Christian father Epiphanius said

Christians had been called Essenes before they adopted the title of Christians.[29]

The doomsday idea was subtly, but tellingly, altered in its passage through these father-worshiping sects with their linear thought patterns, their earthly and heavenly hierarchies, and their militaristic anticipation of the final battle. Though for obvious reasons it is not emphasized today, both Essenic and early Christian doctrines demanded dissolution of the bonds of kin and family, which were still said to be "centered in the blood" of the maternal descent group, and altogether too subject to female influence for patriarchal taste.

Jesus expressed this Essenic doctrine when he said no man could be his disciple "if he hate not his father, and mother, and wife, and children, and brethren, and sisters, yea, and his own life also" (Luke 14:26). Essenes insisted on complete severance of family ties and renunciation of all rights of inheritance, so that any adult who entered their order must turn over all personal property to the order only. (This rule was later applied to great advantage by the Christian church.) Essenes liked to recruit orphans, or young children who had been either abandoned by their parents, or kidnapped from them. Josephus said the Essenes "chose out" other people's children, but it was not clear whether these children were bought, stolen, or voluntarily donated.[30]

According to the priestess's account in the *Völuspá*, all the gods participating in the final battle met death, along with their opponents. Like the ultimate war now being contemplated in our own time, this war left no survivors. By contrast, Persian and Essenic scriptures said only the wicked deities would be destroyed (or alternatively, exiled). The forces of light were supposed to show that for the virtuous, the ultimate battle was survivable.

Essenic hermits firmly believed they would become mighty warriors fighting on the side of the heavenly angels, and would win the warrior's reward of plunder, luxuries, silver and gold, precious stones. The wealth of nations would be brought before them. Kings would bow down to them. All their former enemies would lick the dust from their feet.[31]

It was a revealingly arrogant vision, for men who professed abject humility. Even in its Christian derivative, the Book of Revelation, a similar obsession with riches persisted. The New Jerusalem was to be a realm of incredible wealth, all built with precious jewels. Its occupants would be world rulers who "shall reign for ever and ever" (Rev. 21:18–20, 22:5). Saint Paul even went so far as to promise his followers that, at the last judgment, they would not only pass judgment on their fellow men; they would even judge the angels (1 Cor. 6:3). Significantly, matriarchal cyclic world views never included such blatant greed for wealth and power.

Ironically, the Essenes had originally taken their name from servants of the Goddess. The word *Essene* meant "a drone." It was applied to the eunuch priests of Artemis at her Ephesian temple, where the "drones" accompanied priestesses called *melissae,* "Bees."[32] Like other emasculated priests, such as those devoted to Great Mother Cybele in Phrygia and Rome, these Essenes were thought to have won special holiness by sacrificing their virility to the Goddess's use.

During the reign of Herod, the Essenic community at Qumran was decimated by an earthquake. Buildings were wrecked, and the water cistern cracked, rendering the site uninhabitable.[33] Survivors may have taken the disaster as an early indication of the oncoming last days, and went forth into the outside world to call for universal repentance.

John the Baptist was said to have come from such a community, as did Jesus and Simon Magus. One or more of the Essenic "Christs" might well have undertaken the traditional martyrdom of the sacred king, in the belief that this would insure his own immortality and that of his followers. In the words attributed to Jesus: "Now is the judgment of this world. . . . And I, if I be lifted up from the earth, will draw all men unto me" (John 12:31–32).

Jesus was neither the first nor the last to make such announcements. The final coming of his forerunner Buddha had been expected in the southeast for half a millenium. It was said the world's end would be announced also by a final incarnation of Vishnu, the Kalki Avatara. Persians expected the return of Zoroaster, as Messiah, or the Son of Man, or Yima the Splendid, the Good Shepherd, who met death so men could hope for eternal life. The doomsday story was already very old. It was to get older, for despite continual disproofs and disappointments it would never die out. It is still alive today.

Patriarchal religions particularly emphasized the ideas of conflict, judgment, retribution, separation of the sheep from the goats: the same We-They classification system that always allowed men to see any human opponents as subhuman. Man's universal craving to think himself superior, to belong to an elite group, was nowhere more evident than in doomsday fantasies about the saved and the damned. There were dramatic visions of the elect rising bodily to heavenly bliss under their god's personal supervision, while the sinful majority were dragged screaming into a terrible hell. Gone was the basic message of the Goddess worshipers, that as doomsday Crone she would destroy all the world and all its gods, without distinction, for like death itself she was unselective. Man's version insisted that even death could be evaded, by those who belonged to the right in-group. As for the others, who did not belong, they were "unbelievers" who could be killed with impunity. Followers of male-oriented ideologies have always shown a strong propensity to slaughter those who do not agree with them.

During the early Christian centuries, the "right" in-group was led by church fathers who made celibacy the price of admission to heaven. Some even maintained that the kingdom of God couldn't come at all, until human beings gave up sex, marriage, and propagation. Some of the innermost elite were self-made eunuchs who obeyed Jesus's hint: "There be eunuchs, which have made themselves eunuchs for the kingdom of heaven's sake. He that is able to receive it, let him receive it" (Matt. 19:12). Tertullian repeated this dictum: "The Kingdom of Heaven is thrown open to eunuchs." Justin Martyr proudly boasted that Roman doctors were besieged by Christian men requesting the operation.[34]

In Christianity's first eschatological fervor, it seemed quite unnecessary to propagate a new generation, which would never live to adulthood before the end came. Jesus himself cried woe on pregnant or nursing mothers, who would be especially punished during the last days (Luke 21:23). Thus, Christianity's traditional abhorrence of sex and reproduction began with a vast fear: the fear of death, of dissolution, of being swallowed up in the blackness of cosmic chaos—symbolically, the fear of the Crone.

The power of the Crone lay especially in her ability to destroy gods. The Old Religions considered the Mother's curse the only force capable of bringing death to an "immortal" Heavenly Father;

that is why sacrificial sacred kings, embodying the same Father, were formally cursed before execution. Once the curse was pronounced, the victim's death became inevitable, so no guilt accrued to the executioners. And in a sense it was quite logical for men to invest the Mother of the Gods with the power to destroy those she had created, for any mother could do as much to her children, simply by neglecting them. Similarly, early church fathers feared that women could destroy their God by neglecting him. Any deity consistently ignored by half the human race would inevitably die of a dearth of credibility.

The female principle had always been regarded as both life giver and death bringer. Men therefore believed the ascetic sages such as Essenes, who claimed the only way to rise above the vulnerable mortality of the flesh was to renounce the flesh, thus to renounce mortality with it. Since it was the mother and the Goddess who gave birth to bodies, and woman who provided bodily nourishment and pleasures, a man would have to deny all female powers, such as sexual charisma and motherhood, in order to deny the destructive power of the Crone.

Therefore the fathers said all life born of Eve and her daughters was automatically subject to death. Because sinful Eve brought life into the world, "man born of woman" would have to die, unless male powers of asceticism, more pleasing to the Father God, could intervene. It was considered virtuous for a man to sacrifice his sexuality to the Father, even more than to the Mother, for the hidden sexual rivalry of fathers and sons was as prevalent then as now.

Christian fathers forgot or suppressed earlier scriptures that said it was the mischievous God who cruelly tricked the first man out of eating the fruit of eternal life, by lying to him, claiming the fruit was poisonous.[35] The God of Genesis tried to keep Adam from the fruit of knowledge by making the same false claim, that when he ate the fruit he would die (Gen. 2:17). Even the Bible showed that God's statement was not just false, but conspicuously false: after eating the forbidden fruit, Adam not only did not die, but he lived nearly a thousand years.

The Bible never said the fruit in question was an apple. This idea came from other sources, especially the Aryan tradition that apples from the Tree of Life in the Goddess's magical Western garden of paradise were the food that gave gods their immortality. Whether the place was Avalon, or the Fortunate Isles, or the Hesperides, or Elysium, or Jambu Island; whether the Goddess was Idun, or Hera, or Morgan, or Parvati, or Pomona, or Eve; the idea was the same: She controlled the gift that both men and gods craved above all else. The northern Aryans even considered the Mother's apples essential to the recurrent resurrections or reincarnations they envisioned, and placed vessels of apples in the graves of the dead.[36]

Church fathers suppressed Gnostic writings that said Eve and the serpent were humanity's true saviors, having helped Adam acquire at least some of the knowledge he needed to distinguish good from evil, and having nearly succeeded in winning eternal life for him, against God's express order.[37] But the jealous deity cursed Eve for her efforts. Her failure to win eternal life for her spouse and offspring began to be seen as a direct cause of death for them. And for this, every woman was blamed. Tertullian said every woman was an Eve, the devil's gateway, the deserter of divine law. Because she deserved death, "even the Son of God had to die."[38]

New interpretations were given also to the serpent, a former crony of the Crone, even created by her own hands to be her first consort, according to Egyptian and Mesopotamian sources. Like the Midgard-Worm of Ragnarök, the serpent would lead the forces of darkness in the final battle. But unlike the worm, he would not succeed in killing the God who opposed him. Persians decided that Ahriman the Great Serpent would be defeated yet again; then he and his cohorts would be cast into "outer darkness," or into hell. It might be said that at the last battle they had everything to gain and nothing to lose, if they had already been living throughout the ages in hell.

The Christian version of the doomsday myth made even less sense than its forerunners, but sense was not required of it. It had only to be frightening, to convince the populace that the world was in its terminal age, and no one could survive its death throes except those who went to the right church. The basic change made by patriarchal religions was to claim that doomsday was survivable, therefore that death is survivable, for psychologically they are the same concept.

The symbolism of both doomsday myths and creation myths shows that they are drawn almost literally from the life: that is, from ordinary human experience strained through the mythmaking filter of the collective unconscious. Creation invariably begins with a uterine environment, characterized by darkness, waters, churning movement, "the Deep," and a nondifferentiation of elements, of inner from outer, of self from other. Sometimes there was a suggestion of the fetus contained in the cosmic womb: "When darkness was enveloped in Darkness, then the Mother, the Formless One, Maha-Kali, the Great Power, was one with Maha-Kala, the Absolute."[39] Soon the darkness was pierced by the first light, as a deity said *Fiat lux:* God's phrase was copied from Mother Juno Lucina, who brought the "light" to newborn eyes. It was not necessarily sunlight, just an idea of light. The Bible said the sun was created later, whereas Egyptian scriptures said the sun was born from the Mother's earth-body at the first sunrise.[40]

If creation thus symbolized birth, doomsday could only symbolize the corresponding experience of death. Its imagery suggested destruction of body and mind, convulsions, fevers, chills, suffocation, all kinds of illness and pain projected into the vision of cosmic death. Indeed, subjectively the universe comes into being for each of us at birth, and disappears for each of us at death; and mythology is nothing if not the formalization of the subjective. Each of us has a doomsday in his or her future, no matter what the rest of the world may do or think about it.

The hidden connection between doomsday and the dissolution of the individual, in ordinary death, is plainly shown in the Manichaean hymn called *The Ship of God,* where body and cosmos are interchangeably mingled:

Every hand, link, and shutter of the prison (body) becomes weakened. All the comets quivered, and the stars were whirled about, and each of the planets turned awry in its course. The earth shook, my foundation beneath, and the height of the heavens sank down above. All the rivers, the veins of my body, dried up at their source. All my limbs have connection no longer. . . . The reckoning of my days and months is ended. Harm befell the course of the zodiac's wheel. The seal of my feet and the joints of my toes—each link of the life of my soul was loosed. Each joint of my hands and of my fingers—each was loosed and its seal taken off. All the gristly parts—their life grew feeble. And cold became each one of my limbs.[41]

The idea of the seals probably came from Egypt, where it was thought that the seven souls were sealed to the body at birth by the Seven Heavenly Midwives, emanations of Hathor. Gnostic references to the seals may explain the Gospel Revelation's mysterious allusion to seven seals on the book of life.

Through the centuries, biblical interpreters studied the Book of Revelation, believing its flamboyantly colorful doomsday imagery unique in sacred literature. As a rule, each generation of scholars found allegedly unmistakable references to the age then current, and repeatedly announced the imminence of doomsday, according to the veritable word of God.

This process still continues, as the much-probed Book of Revelation is probed yet again, in search of divine proofs that the world will end in the lifetime of those now living. This particular manifestation of the will to believe has not been scrutinized from a psychological viewpoint, although a true comprehension of the phenomenon might shed considerable light on the mechanisms of human nature.

It is now known that the Book of Revelation was anything but unique. On the contrary, it was just another example of a type of prophecy literature widely popular in the Mediterranean world about the first century A.D. Some of the other pagan or Gnostic examples of the genre were clearly influenced by the concept of the Crone's curse. *On the Origin of the World* gave the classic picture of doomsday brought on by the greed and violence of earthly rulers and their gods, all of them soon to be destroyed by an avenging female spirit:

Kings will be drunk from the flaming sword and they will make war against one another, so that the earth will be drunk from the blood which is poured out. And the seas will be troubled by the war. Then the sun will darken and the moon will lose its light . . . a great thunder will come out of a great power that is above all the powers of Chaos, the place where the firmament of woman is situated. When she had created the first work, she will take off her wise flame of insight. She will put on a senseless wrath. Then she will drive out the gods of Chaos whom she created together with the First Father. She will cast them down to the abyss. They will be wiped out by their own injustice . . . they will gnaw at one another until they are destroyed by their First Father. When he destroys them, he will turn against himself and destroy himself until he ceases to be. And their heavens will fall upon one another and their powers will burn.[42]

About 500 B.C., ascetic Buddhist monks began teaching that the death/doomsday brought on by the Mother's curse might be avoided, if a man could totally identify himself with an eternal, guiltless God, immortal by definition. Having postulated such a God, they insisted that their ascetic denial of the needs of the earthly, mother-given body would make them become this God, and that the supreme goal of their existence was to realize fully that self and God were one and the same.[43]

This Buddhist idea was also developed by mystery cults of the early Christian era, including the Christian mysteries themselves. In the worship of Osiris, Mithra, Hermes, Orpheus, Christ, and many other savior-gods, doomsday myths were used as warnings against the final destruction of the self which could be saved, after all, through identification with the saving deity. Such was the ultimate purpose of the mystagogues' ascetic practices, sacraments, and litanies.

Cicero said initiation into the pagan Mysteries made a man become God, "in no whit inferior" to the deities in heaven. Epictetus and Seneca spoke of the Holy Spirit dwelling within the initiate. Hermetists said they were deified in fact when their rites made them the image (eidolon) of their deity. Mithraists used the same verbal formula later attributed to Jesus, saying God lives in the enlightened man, and the man in God. Clement of Alexandria said the whole revelation of the Logos, or Christ, meant that man might become God for the sake of his immortality: "The true Christian Gnostic has already become God."[44]

These curious expressions of worldwide male megalomania place the God concept in its true source, the mind of man; they are one and the same after all. The philosophers' idea that the universe cannot exist unless God is present to perceive it is only another form of the doomsday wish that all the world should cease to be once the individual has ceased to be conscious of it.

Such a psychological version of the doomsday idea is not tenable by the rational mind, since it is self-evident that people die and the universe goes on undisturbed. Nevertheless, man in his hubris eternally rejects this reality in relation to himself. He persuades himself that if enough men can be found to agree on the unrealistic notion of personal immortality, though it be realized only in human words, then man may believe that by his Logos (Word) he creates eternal life for himself in fact.

Hence, men tell each other that they can survive death/doomsday. Repeated often enough, this becomes an article of faith. It is now *the* article of faith; it is what is meant by salvation. Though the whole world/body may collapse and dissolve away, still the "I," because it is divine, must endure forever. "I" will know everything. "I" will be infinitely blessed. "I" will be an indestructible, immortal soul, like God. In effect, "I" will be God. Thus the worshiper of Osiris, as he ate his god in the form of sacramental bread and wine, declared himself one with the deity of light and truth, eternal as Osiris himself, even sharing his title of God of Gods.[45]

As the only animal to know that he will cease to be, man escapes this knowledge with the aid of a rather amazing mental construction, for which he has never found any empirical evidence, but which he nevertheless continues to elaborate and develop. Though the true source of this massive cultural effort has not been identified, its driving force is obviously very powerful—perhaps even powerful enough to create the doomsday that man has so long desired, now that the physical means of doing so at last lie in his hands.

Can it be possible that presumably sane men would undertake to destroy all the life on their mother planet, because they can't bear the thought of dying alone, as every other creature does?

Opposing nations now threaten each other with incredible destruction, despite the fact that the proposed holocaust would probably destroy the instigators as well as their enemies. Thus we are faced with a logical absurdity. The threat can't operate as a deterrent, unless it is taken seriously by both sides, which means that both sides must be willing to carry it out. So, in the final analysis, the threat cannot deter what it is supposed to deter. Or, to put it another way, we must be willing to destroy ourselves in order to escape destruction.

The human species has impaled itself on the horns of many a mad dilemma in the past; but this is surely one of the maddest yet:

the end product of "rational" male leadership and technological progress.

It should be noted that this dilemma is one of the few social phenomena in which humanity's female half took no part whatever. It is entirely the creation of men.[46]

Moreover, men only have participated for three decades in countless meetings and plans aimed at disarmament and world peace—with the result that, today, the threat of world war is worse than ever. One can only conclude that what powerful men say they want is not what they really want. One is reminded of the men's God, who talked a good case about his universal love for all *Man* kind, yet unhesitatingly hurled a vast majority of his loved ones into a hell of eternal torture, for the sake of an original sin they had not even personally committed.

In the sum total of human intelligence, the conventional view of the so-called male mind as its logical component seems hardly tenable. What passes for male logic must be laid aside, if we as a species can ever come to the plain realization that death/doomsday is not survivable; that none of us ever have, nor ever will, outlive the Crone's inevitable curse in time; and that none of us will enjoy any godlike victory in the international holocaust now being planned for us by our (exclusively male) leaders.

If one wants to search ancient writings for prophecies of present doom, the Sybilline Books of Rome's pagan priestesses might do as well as any Christian or Gnostic source, since they contain much the same material. One such book presented a picture very like the possibilities being contemplated in today's "man's world":

A murky cloud shall cover the boundless earth from east and west and north and south. And then a great river of burning fire shall flow down from heaven and consume every place, earth and great ocean and the grey-blue sea, lakes and rivers . . . and ashes shall cover all things.[47]

8

The Future Crone

The Future Crone

8

Not only is a real doomsday possible at the present time, its possibility is entirely subject to the thoughts and actions of human males. Men have achieved the ultimate power, as they understand power: they have the capability of destroying absolutely everything, including themselves, in a gaudy funeral pyre to try to challenge the brilliance of the sun or to impress the uncaring stars. Can hubris aspire any higher?

The modern world is ruled largely by men of middle age and older. Though such individuals may be qualified for leadership in business and politics by reason of their career experiences, as a group they may be the least qualified psychologically to make vital decisions on behalf of their entire species.

Among other social animals, mature males must constantly defend their claims to territory and females against the challenges of younger males. The life of a "dominant" male is a study in insecurity. He must succeed in intimidating or physically defeating every rival, even—or especially—when he is in a weakened condition, or otherwise disinclined to fight. Should he become sick, or too old to win his battles any more, he is soon replaced by a stronger specimen. Thus nature insures that male breeding stock will consist only of the fittest.

The same biological imperatives must govern the deeper instincts of human beings, too. However, the complexities of civilization have given older human males many ways to consolidate their power against encroachment by younger, more virile rivals. Patriarchal civilization may be viewed as a network of defense measures to alleviate the fundamental insecurities of the mature male. Monomogamous marriage is one of the defense measures that allow older males to feel safe from such encroachment, and this is why female adultery has been considered a crime almost as culpable as murder.

Paradoxical as it may sound, one of the most effective of men's defense measures has always been war. War offers an excellent excuse for older males to bind younger ones firmly to their service, and not incidentally, to destroy a good many of them in the process. Best of all, responsibility for their destruction can be laid on the enemy leaders. In effect, elder males of both warring nations can safely and blamelessly exterminate each other's younger rivals. At the same time, each plays the gambling game that can earn more territory for their own greater glory. War leaders can feel themselves admired, effective, and powerful in ways that are seldom possible in times of peace. War is the ultimate male ego trip.

Some ego satisfactions also filter down to the younger males who play the part of sacrificial victims. They too can find ways to feel powerful, even though they dare not challenge their own rulers. Through loot and rape, the traditional prerogatives of the warrior, they can augment the minimal rewards their leaders give them. The frustration of their social powerlessness can be relieved by various defusing mechanisms, such as redirected aggression, support of the in-group, and manipulation of weaponry, which extends into adulthood the remembered pleasure of little boys playing with toy guns. For many men, war experiences represent the high point of their lives. Nothing else will ever seem so dramatic or exciting.

Men's gods, even when nominally in favor of peace and opposed to killing, have always been quick to suspend their own rules in time of war, to unite with their worshipers in hatred of the enemy (even when the enemy worships the same God, and believes he is on *their* side), and to condone any degree of violence. There is no such thing as a male god consistently insistent on loving one's enemies, nor even on respecting the so-called human rights of others. In war, the others are automatically nonhuman.

Historically, the most aggressive, cruel, and exploitive men in the world have been Christians, who used the very word *Christian* as a synonym for the virtues of peace and love, yet managed not to see the incongruity of their own behavior and their deity's self-contradiction. Even today, Christians like to remark that there are no atheists in foxholes, conveniently overlooking the fact that if Christianity were truly a religion of nonaggression, there would be no Christians in foxholes either.

The consolations of religion have never been withheld from soldiers on the ground that they are engaged in the sin of killing. Churches do not criticize the military. Funeral services are not denied those responsible for political massacres. The bloodiest tyrants, the most sadistic oppressors, even men engaged in organized crime, can buy the full panoply of religion's guarantees of God's indulgence.

"Jealous" father gods have always fostered wars as massive rituals of male jealousy, in which the father's fathomless hostility toward the son/supplanter is given formal expression. Not incidentally, wars bring a hefty share of the spoils into church treasuries, in return for divine assistance. Just as medieval monastic orders founded on an alleged vow of poverty usually managed to become very rich in a very short time, so also the alleged Prince of Peace has been one of the most warlike of deities for more than fifteen hundred years. "Holy wars" tend to be especially vicious, since they especially emphasize the We/They dichotomy that is man's preferred view of his own fellow creatures.

It seems clear that gods are merely additional weapons in the struggle of male leaders to stay "on top," by lending divine sanction to whatever it is the leaders want done, and by threatening possible insurgents with divine retribution. "God's laws" are always in strict alignment with the interests of the ruling caste. When their interests change, so do God's orders.

Religious images may be no more than projections of the human imagination, but they have evident effects on human behavior, in the manner of a feedback loop. Change in social patterns produces change in the deity. Conversely, a change in the divine image can produce social change. However imaginary they may be, religious images matter.

Centuries ago, European men learned to beat their wives because their God, through the mouths of his priests, assured them that it was right and proper to do so. For themselves, priests assured each other that God commanded them not only to beat, but even to torture and burn women and children. Similarly, in ancient times when the Goddess encouraged sexual sacraments in her honor to enhance general fertility, sex was universally viewed as a holy communion and not as a sin.

Perhaps the world would benefit by a well-considered restoration of the feminine divine image to something like its former preeminence, if for no other reason than the hope of abolishing man's favorite game of war from our endangered planet. This game has gone too far and is no longer amusing. Women have never liked it, because they do not derive similar satisfactions from it.

On the contrary, war strikes at the very root of the feminine psyche, in its disruption of family life, its permission of vandalism and destruction, its imposition of unnecessary suffering on the helpless. Women know literally in their guts, in a way that men will never know, how much unremitting effort goes into the creation of a mammalian life, through all the years from conception to adulthood. Even women who have never been parents often seem to understand these matters better than many men who have been. Sane people do not heedlessly destroy anything that takes so long to build, even when it belongs to someone else. Women are less easily persuaded by the We/They dichotomy, and more prone to sympathize with the basic humanness, vulnerability, and personal uniqueness of other human beings.

To envision a deity in the true female tradition, it is necessary to purge the image of simplistic or unrealistic male interpretations. For example, men's favorite "sex goddess" figure is useless, because she is not empowering for women; she only represents abject acquiescence to male lusts. The "virgin mother" figure is little better. Not only has her sexuality been amputated, but she shows cognizance of only one brief stage in woman's experience of life, and even that cognizance is based on a biological impossibility. It may be that a truly powerful female image can be found only in prepatriarchal traditions of the complete trinitarian life cycle: Virgin, Mother, Crone. Especially the Crone.

As Destroyer, the Crone approximates what men can understand as real power: the power to destroy. As Death, the Crone forces recognition of biological fact opposed to religious fantasy. Her worshipers long ago believed in the psychic necessity of learning to look upon her ugliness without fear, so as to learn to love and comfort those made ugly by approaching death, and to help them accept the inevitable by not showing one's own fear. The function of the dakini was lost by patriarchy, yet it was a vital function, and its loss is felt. Male clergy have not been as effective in dealing with death as the priestesses who preceded them.

Naturally, the Crone also represented the life-affirming moral wisdom of elder women, as opposed to the power-seeking defensiveness of elder men. As the summation of feminine life experience, she was seen as a healer and teacher, as well as a death bringer. She could pity weakness, foster creativity, or punish violence. She was Mother's Mother, the ultimate authority for the children of earth.

When the Crone was recognized as a valid image, the old woman was not seen as a useless object, as she often is today. Beyond her sexual and maternal functions, she had others, perhaps even more important. She commanded respect. Her advice was sought. Her community looked up to her and took her ideas seriously.

Moreover, the Crone was not so inclined to break her own laws as the inconsistent gods of men. According to her word, karma was karma: one who injures will be injured; one who is kind will receive kindness. The golden rule was her idea, in India and in ancient Egypt, long before it was copied into the Gospels. She was implacable; she couldn't be bought off like her sons the gods. Like nature, she was not to be manipulated by flattery or impressed by puny human words. One had to learn to exist within her framework, not in opposition to it, for this was only common sense. Who would plant in the season of harvest, or who could expect to win love by hateful behavior?

Most of all, the Crone can represent precisely the kind of power women so desperately need today, and do not have: the power to force men to do what is right, for the benefit of future generations and of the earth itself. Forcing seems to be necessary. Men do not voluntarily relinquish their ego trips, war toys, and money games. Like spoiled children, many men push selfish behavior as far as they can, perhaps secretly trying to reach the point where Mother will clamp down and say "No more," and mean it.

But when they have been at pains to deprive Mother of all her power through so many centuries, who is left to discipline them to peace? Certainly not superhero Father. Since men define power as the capacity to destroy, then the Destroying Mother must be the most powerful female image for them, therefore the only one likely to force them in any new direction. As feminists have discovered, men may dislike angry female voices but they will listen to them, whereas the sweet voices are not even heard.

Metaphors like these take on practical meaning in women's capacity to see through men's pretenses and to reject men's self-serving images. Men feared the judgmental eye of the wisewoman even when she was socially powerless. This, then, is the chink in the armor of patriarchal establishments. When many women together say no and mean it, the whole structure can collapse.

Women who join together with each other to deny the male God who cursed their sex and to reject his demands for obedience, praise, service, and money, automatically free themselves from one of the most potent psychological traps men ever set for them. Without God to tell them that they must serve and obey abusive husbands, their fetters turn to sand, and they can step away from what seemed a prison. Without God to order them to bear children they don't want, they take personal control of their bodies. Without God to call them guilty for experiencing sexual pleasure, they gain new confidence and trust in their own physicality. And if the world's women joined together to reinstate a full three-dimensional feminine divinity, with her own authentic theology, life on our planet might be quite different.

Such a view of future possibilities must be accompanied by certain caveats. Opposing or replacing a male-oriented religion by a female-oriented one certainly would not solve all social problems overnight, any more than women's winning the vote could solve them. And there would always be the danger that success would attract male greed all over again.

The history of religion in the Western world offers one of the best examples of men's propensity to harness the religious impulse to the service of their own greed. This history also proves that there is no limit to the atrocities men will commit in the interest of that greed. These things must not be forgotten.

Then there are philosophical questions, such as, if God is not real, how can the Goddess be any more so? We live in a scientific age, which quite properly demands empirical proof for external phenomena. We can no longer be so naive as to envision any deity actually existing "out there," somewhere in space (or possibly around it), watching us with real eyes, reacting to us with real human-type emotions, becoming annoyed with us if we neglect our little offerings and devotions. We know this kind of image is childish.

We know that "sacred scriptures" are the works of men, and usually of ignorant men, at that. We know that fiery hells populated by sadistic demons are only our nursery nightmares. We know that our world did not begin a mere six thousand years ago with the sudden creation of a single man and woman. Having outgrown such foolish beliefs, we can't return to a former state of credulity. How can any deity survive our enlightenment?

Yet we also know that our myth symbols are like waking dreams, our best and perhaps only keys to much-needed self-comprehension, both individual and collective. We can talk to and about deities "as if" they were real, using their myths to show ourselves the way to our own motives, impulses, faults, fears, and guilts. Psychology finds the study of religions a rich source of insight. A brain can be dissected in the laboratory, but a mind can be dissected only *in vivo,* using symbols in lieu of scalpels. Much of our psychological subjective "truth" is deposited in religious or mythic coffers. And these can be opened by the wisdom of the Crone.

The wisdom of the Crone is that mysterious quality men like to call "feminine intuition" to avoid using its real name: intelligence. Like other female animals, genetically prepared to be responsible for lives other than their own, women are quick learners and keen observers. With the cumulative experience of many years of living, observing, and relating to others, women may routinely achieve higher levels of understanding the human condition than most men dream of.

When a rare man does achieve a comparable sensitivity, he is often hailed as a genius. After all, what made the figure of Jesus so charismatic to fifty generations? Not his scourging of merchants; not his impossible miracles; not his false prophecy of doomsday; not even his alleged Godhood; but chiefly his "feminine" qualities of understanding and kindness—to say nothing of self-sacrifice—which any woman is expected to exhibit (and usually does) every ordinary day of her life.

If the self-seeking powerlust of mature men were made subject to the "intuitive" judgment of mature women, instead of the other way round, surely human life and society could be improved. The earth might become a safer, kinder, healthier place. People might care more for the welfare of future generations. Instead of trying to escape inevitable death in futile fantasies, they might enrich life by honest work on their legacy to their posterity.

Women, who have suffered so much at the hands of patriarchal mythmakers, need no longer pretend not to understand their motives. God can't, but woman can call man to account for his gynocidal, genocidal behavior.

She had better do it soon, for he is already counting down to doomsday.

Notes

Most works cited in the notes are identified by author rather than by title. When more than one work by one author is cited, the note includes both the author's name and an abbreviated title.

2. THE LOST CRONE

1. Rawson, *E. A.*, 260.
2. Janssen-Jurreit, 308.
3. Edwardes, 45.
4. Gifford, 143.
5. Graves, *G. M.* 1:206.
6. *Assyrian and Babylonian Literature,* 338–39.
7. Lederer, 126.
8. Janssen-Jurreit, 312.
9. Bullough, 114.
10. Malvern, 30; Tennant, 207, 244.
11. H. Smith, 238.
12. Cavendish, 28.
13. Hauswirth, 30.
14. de Riencourt, 167.
15. Rawson, *A. T.,* 184; *E. A.,* 159.
16. Ashe, 151; de Riencourt, 150.
17. *Encyclopedia Britannica,* S.V. "Ephesus."
18. Lederer, 141; Mahanirvanatantra, 127.
19. Graves, *G. M.* 1:52.
20. Legman, 650.
21. Frazer, 412.
22. Ashe, 135.
23. Malvern, 39.
24. Mâle, 235.
25. Ashe, 112, 185.
26. Graves, *W. G.,* 411.
27. Ashe, 48.
28. Briffault, 3:97.
29. Budge, *G. E.* 2:253.
30. *Larousse,* 77.
31. Hyde, 111.
32. O'Flaherty, 68.
33. Massa, 101.
34. Mahanirvanatantra, 12, 53, 56, 177.
35. Mahanirvanatantra, 295–96.
36. de Riencourt, 165.
37. Lindsay, 75, 120.
38. Avalon, 517.
39. Graves, *G. M.* 1:27.
40. Budge, *G. E.* 1:473.
41. *Larousse,* 203–4.
42. H. R. E. Davidson, 229.
43. Loomis, 387.
44. Angus, 12.
45. Castiglioni, 253; Robbins, 102.
46. Boulding, 554.
47. Scot, 5.
48. Wendt, 137.
49. Boulding, 185.
50. King, 38.
51. Melamed, 163.
52. Campbell, *Oc. M.,* 86, 153.
53. See Fast.
54. Stimpson & Person, 78.
55. Haskell, 178–79.
56. Evans-Wentz, 203, 356.
57. Barnstone, 588.

3. THE WISE CRONE

1. Campbell, *P. M.,* 129.
2. Mahanirvanatantra, 103.
3. Budge, *G. E.* 2:89, 100.
4. Scott, 192–93.

5. Lindsay, 106.
6. Campbell, *M. I.,* 156.
7. Graves, *G. M.* 1:118.
8. Gifford, 42; Edwardes, 93.
9. Brasch, 55; Montagu, 243; Campbell, *P. M.,* 103.
10. Briffault, 2:416.
11. Walker, S.V. "menstrual blood."
12. Gifford, 26.
13. *Larousse,* 54.
14. Bachofen, 189.
15. Briffault, 2:493.
16. Gilligan, 17, 173.
17. Pritchard 1, 31, 132.
18. Budge, *D. N.,* 159; *G. E.* 2:300.
19. Budge, *G. E.* 1:286.
20. Budge, D.N., 20.
21. Budge, *D. N.,* 254; Hallet, 411.
22. Barrett, 143, 217–19.
23. Robinson, 176.
24. *Encyclopedia Britannica,* S.V. "Byblos."
25. Branston, 30.
26. Branston, 88.
27. Spence, *E. O.,* 409.
28. Wedeck, 140.
29. Turville-Petre, 150.
30. Wimberly, 219.
31. Malory, 2:179, 199.
32. Rees, 145.
33. Scot, 550.
34. Russell, 16.
35. Sturluson, 39.
36. Wimberly, 36.
37. Hazlitt, 296.
38. Bachofen, 215; Walker, S.V. "kingship."
39. Briffault, 1:416; Hartley, 127.
40. *Assyrian and Babylonian Literature,* 91, 114, 130.
41. Joyce, 1:278.
42. Harding, 41.
43. Briffault, 3:80.
44. Budge, *A. T.,* 52.
45. Campbell, *Oc. M.,* 443.
46. *Assyrian and Babylonian Literature,* 120.
47. de Riencourt, 193.
48. Vermaseren, 22.
49. *Encyclopedia Britannica,* S.V. "meteorites."

50. Frazer, 404 et seq.
51. *Larousse,* 37.
52. Graves, *G. M.* 1:44–45.
53. Wendt, 52, 66; Sobol, 153–55.
54. Graves, *W. G.,* 244.
55. Knight, *S. L.,* 130.
56. Budge, *G. E.* 1:459.
57. Budge, *E. L.,* 55.
58. Neumann, pl. 87, 111–12.
59. Gifford, 63.
60. Gifford, 26, 47.
61. Elworthy, 195.
62. Zimmer, 25.
63. Avalon, 172, 388.
64. Bullough, 105; Sadock, Kaplan, and Freedman, 23.
65. Robinson, 104.
66. Pagels, 57–58.
67. Pagels, 30–31.
68. Robinson, 176–78.
69. Jonas, 72, 98.
70. Wilkins, 112.
71. Barnstone, 16.
72. Patai, 139, 148–49.
73. Collins, 54, 220.
74. Jonas, 218.
75. Patai, 178.
76. Stone, 131.
77. Patai, 147; Barnstone, 29–30.
78. Mahanirvanatantra, xxiv.
79. *Larousse,* 207.
80. Walker, 484, 587.
81. Barnstone, 64–65, 75, 658.
82. Graves, *W. G.,* 144.
83. Joyce, 1:261–62.
84. Waddell, 233, 361.
85. Evans-Wentz, 157.
86. Boulding, 193–94; Graves, *W. G.,* 256.
87. Walker, 387.
88. Greeley, 36.
89. Rich, 67.

4. THE TERRIBLE CRONE

1. Neumann, 149–53.
2. Wilson, 257.
3. de Riencourt, 167.
4. Avalon, 27.
5. Mahanirvanatantra, 47–50.
6. Rawson, *A. T.,* 184.

7. Rawson, *E. A.*, 159.
8. Avalon, 396.
9. Menen, 149.
10. Rawson, *A. T.*, 112.
11. Avalon, 533, 171.
12. *Encyclopedia Britannica*, S.V. "Kali."
13. Waddell, 129.
14. Tatz and Kent, 148.
15. Bardo Thodol, 128.
16. Spence, *E. O.*, 165.
17. Eliade, 76–78.
18. Lederer, 127.
19. Rawson, *E. A.*, 152.
20. *Larousse*, 306.
21. Mahanirvanatantra, 295–96.
22. Trigg, 186.
23. Frazer, 467; Joyce, 1:316.
24. Rees, 41; Spence, *E. O.*, 199.
25. Rees, 193.
26. Tatz and Kent, 84.
27. Campbell, *P. M.*, 333.
28. Squire, 413.
29. Spence, *E. O.*, 354.
30. Turville-Petre, 206, 231.
31. Malvern, 117.
32. Joyce, 1:352.
33. Campbell, *Or. M.*, 307–8.
34. Eliade, 385.
35. Goodrich, 236; Shah, 335.
36. Dumézil, 296–97.
37. Rawson, *E. A.*, 160; Silberer, 280.
38. Lethaby, 238.
39. Avalon, 328.
40. Wedeck, 66.
41. Whitehouse, 60.
42. Gimbutas, 224.
43. Goodrich, 63–66.
44. Spence, *H. O. D.*, 56.
45. Miles, 93.
46. Rawson, *E. A.*, 30.
47. Scott, 239–43.
48. Turville-Petre, 72.
49. Spence, *H. O. D.*, 111.
50. Hazlitt, 25.
51. Knight, *D. W. P.*, 170.
52. Avalon, 318.
53. Ruether, 143–44.
54. Avalon, 518.
55. Mahanirvanatantra, 295.

56. Cavendish, 88.
57. Gimbutas, 102.
58. Book of the Dead, 161–63.
59. Branston, 208.
60. Legge, 1:183.
61. *Larousse*, 323.
62. Seligmann, 14.
63. Wainwright, 113; Turville-Petre, 55.
64. Miles, 242.
65. Rank, 73.
66. Steenstrup, 149.
67. Knight, *D. W. P.*, 78.
68. Cavendish, 88.
69. Branston, 96–97.
70. Woods, 156.
71. Guerber, 274–75.
72. Lethaby, 163.
73. Branston, 164.
74. Turville-Petre, 164.
75. Turville-Petre, 257.
76. Kramer and Sprenger, 121.
77. Campbell, *Oc. M.*, 352.
78. Hallet, 368.
79. Spence, *E. O.*, 297.
80. Turville-Petre, 48, 56.
81. Angus, 154.
82. Baring-Gould, 620.
83. Steenstrup, 104.
84. Spence, *H. O. D.*, 37.
85. Kramer and Sprenger, 47.
86. Melamed, 40, 56, 94.
87. Walker, 919.
88. Barnstone, 441.
89. Greeley, 89.

5. THE CRONE AND THE CAULDRON

1. Goodrich, 18, 32.
2. Gaster, 764.
3. Goodrich, 45–47.
4. Angus, 12; Gifford, 55.
5. Cumont, 86.
6. Miles, 181.
7. Cavendish, 82.
8. Hazlitt, 379.
9. Trigg, 80.
10. Branston, 53, 82; Turville-Petre, 246.

11. Campbell, *Or. M.*, 182.
12. *Assyrian and Babylonian Literature*, 308.
13. Book of the Dead, 114.
14. Graves, *G.M.* 2:27.
15. Gaster, 587.
16. Briffault, 1:486.
17. Herodotus, 390.
18. Wendt, 137.
19. Dumézil, 213, 243.
20. Robertson, 115.
21. Walker, S.V. "dog."
22. Eliade, 41, 159, 237, 439.
23. Baroja, 59.
24. Keightley, 295.
25. Graves, *W. G.*, 409.
26. de Santillana and von Dechend, 383.
27. Gaster, 787.
28. H. R. E. Davidson, 129–130.
29. Stewart, 80–82.
30. Barrett, 92; Angus, 71.
31. Graves, *G.M.* 1:72.
32. de Santillana and von Dechend, 107.
33. *Larousse*, 300–304.
34. Briffault, 3:451.
35. Malory, 1:xxi.
36. *Encyclopedia Britannica*, S.V. "Glastonbury."
37. Spence, *E. O.*, 246.
38. Weston, 71–72.
39. Weston, 171.
40. *Assyrian and Babylonian Literature*, 120.
41. Shah, 319.
42. Avalon, 517.
43. Mahanirvanatantra, 47–50.
44. Massa, 101.
45. Ruether, 235.
46. de Riencourt, 23.
47. Ruether, 258.
48. Amberson and Smith, 29.
49. Jung, 232–38.
50. Budge, *E. M.*, 20.
51. Jung and von Franz, 143.
52. Briffault, 2:605; Angus, 173.
53. Wedeck, 203.
54. de Lys, 139–41.
55. Miles, 242.
56. d'Alviella, 183.
57. Shumaker, 178, 183.
58. Robinson, 462, 467.
59. Collins, 54, 220.
60. Jung, 377–79.
61. Angus, 207.
62. Darrah, 77–79.
63. Scot, 340–42.
64. Joyce, 2:375.
65. Evans-Wentz, 147.
66. Spence, 252.

6. THE CRONE TURNS WITCH

1. Summers, 486–87.
2. H. Smith, 292–93.
3. Lea, 20.
4. Lea, 173–75, 224–25.
5. Robbins, 8.
6. de Lys, 458.
7. Keightley, 422, 427, 431–32.
8. Borchardt, 282.
9. Rees, 145; Malory, 2:179, 199.
10. White, 2:36; Briffault, 1:488.
11. Lederer, 150; Agrippa, 270.
12. Ewen, 69.
13. Kramer and Sprenger, 66.
14. White, 2:63.
15. Dumézil, 37, 616.
16. Robbins, 157.
17. Dreifus, 7.
18. Tuchman, 216.
19. Scot, 20.
20. Baroja, 126.
21. de Reincourt, 227.
22. Bullough, 177.
23. J. H. Smith, 241.
24. Scot, 227, 248.
25. Kramer and Sprenger, 44.
26. T. Davidson, 99.
27. Scot, 405.
28. Phillips, 180.
29. Bromberg, 59.
30. Plaidy, 157.
31. Kramer and Sprenger, 79.
32. Coulton, 18–20; H. Smith, 206.
33. Miles, 270.
34. Lea, 60, 97, 257.
35. Gornick & Moran, 154–55.
36. Boulding, 554.
37. Ewen, 251–53.
38. Haining, 77.

39. Robbins, 385, 464.
40. O'Flaherty, 68.
41. H. Smith, 238.
42. Tennant, 207, 244.
43. Robinson, 141.
44. Janssen-Jurreit, 317.
45. Pearsall, 190; Hazlitt, 158; Robbins, 359.
46. Rich, 213.
47. Kramer and Sprenger, xliii, 121.
48. Scot, 4–5, 40.
49. Keightley, 431.
50. Murstein, 227.
51. Hartman and Banner, 31.
52. Hobbs, 90–92.
53. Rich, 183.
54. Bromberg, 60, 197.
55. Castiglioni, 165.
56. Scot, 141.
57. Spence, 345.
58. Bullough, 163.
59. Daly, 183, 200–201.
60. Lea, 224.
61. Spence, 354.

7. THE DOOMSDAY CRONE

1. Branston, 289–92.
2. Hooke, M. E. M., 112.
3. Branston, 293.
4. Mahanirvanatantra, 295.
5. Branston, 200.
6. Branston, 285.
7. Larousse, 285.
8. Potter and Sargent, 174.
9. Branston, 277.
10. Squire, 118.
11. Mahanirvanatantra, xlvii–xlviii.

12. Turville-Petre, 79.
13. Tennant, 134.
14. Cavendish, 128.
15. Zimmer, 15.
16. Mahanirvanatantra, 12.
17. Zimmer, 35–36.
18. Campbell, Oc. M., 196.
19. Hooke, S. P., 89.
20. Cumont, 61.
21. O'Flaherty, 339.
22. Joyce, 1:517.
23. Larousse, 317.
24. Black, 3.
25. Pfeifer, 51.
26. Larousse, 315.
27. Albright, 232.
28. Pfeifer, 133.
29. Doane, 426.
30. Pfeifer, 59, 138.
31. Pfeifer, 82.
32. Gimbutas, 183.
33. Pfeifer, 24.
34. Lederer, 162; Briffault, 3:372.
35. Hooke, M. E. M., 57–58.
36. Turville-Petre, 187; Hollander, 39.
37. Jonas, 95, 204; Malvern, 34; Pagels, 31.
38. Bullough, 114.
39. de Riencourt, 165.
40. Budge, G. E. 1:473.
41. Barnstone, 321.
42. Barnstone, 74.
43. Walker, 850.
44. Angus, 102–112.
45. Angus, 139; Book of the Dead, 650.
46. Boulding, 761.
47. Barnstone, 558.

Bibliography

Agrippa, Henry Cornelius. *The Philosophy of Natural Magic.* Secaucus, N.J.: University Books, 1974.

Albright, William Powell. *Yahweh and the Gods of Canaan.* New York: Doubleday, 1968.

Amberson, William R., and Dietrich C. Smith. *Outline of Physiology.* Baltimore: Williams & Wilkins, 1948.

Angus, S. *The Mystery-Religions.* New York: Dover, 1975.

Ashe, Geoffrey. *The Virgin.* London: Routledge & Kegan Paul, 1976.

Assyrian and Babylonian Literature, Selected Translations. New York: D. Appleton & Co., 1901.

Avalon, Arthur. *Shakti and Shakta.* New York: Dover, 1978.

Bachofen, J. J. *Myth, Religion, and Mother Right.* Princeton, N.J.: Princeton University Press, 1967.

Bardo Thodol. Translated by W. Y. Evans-Wentz. London: Oxford University Press, 1927.

Baring-Gould, Sabine. *Curious Myths of the Middle Ages.* New York: University Books, 1967.

Barnstone, Willis, ed. *The Other Bible.* San Francisco: Harper & Row, 1984.

Baroja, Julio Caro. *The World of the Witches.* Chicago: University of Chicago Press, 1965.

Barrett, C. K. *The New Testament Background.* New York: Harper & Row, 1961.

Black, Matthew. *The Scrolls and Christian Origins.* New York: Scribner, 1961.

Book of the Dead. Translated by E. A. Wallis Budge. New York: Bell Publishing Co., 1960.

Borchardt, Frank. *German Antiquity in Renaissance Myth.* Baltimore: Johns Hopkins University Press, 1971.

Boulding, Elise. *The Underside of History.* Boulder: Westview Press, 1976.

Branston, Brian. *Gods of the North.* London: Thames & Hudson, 1955.

Brasch, R. *How Did Sex Begin?* New York: McKay, 1973.

Briffault, Robert. *The Mothers.* 3 vols. New York: Macmillan, 1927.

Bromberg, Walter. *From Shaman to Psychotherapist.* Chicago: Henry Regnery Co., 1975.

Budge, Sir E. A. Wallis. *Amulets and Talismans.* New York: University Books, 1968.

———. *Gods of the Egyptians.* 2 vols. New York: Dover, 1969.

———. *Egyptian Magic.* New York: Dover, 1971.

———. *Dwellers on the Nile.* New York: Dover, 1977.

————. *Egyptian Language.* New York: Dover, 1977.

Bullough, Vern L. *The Subordinate Sex.* Chicago: University of Illinois Press, 1973.

Campbell, Joseph. *Primitive Mythology.* New York: Viking Press, 1959.

————. *Oriental Mythology.* New York: Viking Press, 1962.

————. *Occidental Mythology.* New York: Viking Press, 1964.

————. *The Mythic Image.* Princeton, N.J.: Princeton University Press, 1974.

Castiglioni, Arturo. *Adventures of the Mind.* New York: Knopf, 1946.

Cavendish, Richard. *The Powers of Evil.* New York: Putnam, 1975.

Collins, Joseph B. *Christian Mysticism in the Elizabethan Age.* New York: Octagon Books, 1971.

Coulton, G. G. *Inquisition and Liberty.* Boston: Beacon Press, 1959.

Cumont, Franz. *Astrology and Religion Among the Greeks and Romans.* New York: Dover, 1960.

d'Alviella, Count Goblet. *The Migration of Symbols.* New York: University Books, 1956.

Daly, Mary. *Gyn/Ecology: The Metaethics of Radical Feminism.* Boston: Beacon Press, 1978.

Darrah, John. *The Real Camelot: Paganism and the Arthurian Romances.* London: Thames & Hudson, 1981.

Davidson, H. R. Ellis. *Gods and Myths of the Viking Age.* New York: Bell Publishing Co., 1981.

Davidson, Terry. *Conjugal Crime.* New York: Hawthorn Books, 1978.

de Lys, Claudia. *The Giant Book of Superstitions.* Secaucus, N.J.: Citadel Press, 1979.

de Riencourt, Amaury. *Sex and Power in History.* New York: Dell, 1974.

de Santillana, Giorgio, and Hertha von Dechend. *Hamlet's Mill: An Essay on Myth and the Frame of Time.* Boston: Gambit, 1969.

Doane, T. W. *Bible Myths and Their Parallels in Other Religions.* New York: University Books, 1971.

Dreifus, Claudia, ed. *Seizing Our Bodies.* New York: Vintage Books, 1978.

Dumézil, Georges. *Archaic Roman Religion.* 2 vols. Chicago: University of Chicago Press, 1970.

Edwardes, Allen. *The Jewel in the Lotus.* New York: Lancer Books, 1965.

Eliade, Mircea. *Shamanism.* Princeton, N.J.: Princeton University Press, Bollingen Series, 1964.

Elworthy, Frederick. *The Evil Eye.* New York: Julian Press, 1958.

Encyclopedia Britannica, 3d ed., 1970.

Evans-Wentz, W. Y. *The Fairy-Faith in Celtic Countries.* New York: University Books, 1966.

Ewen, C. L'Estrange. *Witchcraft and Demonianism.* London: Heath Cranton Ltd., 1933.

Fast, Julius. *The Incompatibility of Men and Women and How To Overcome It.* New York: M. Evans & Co., 1971.

Frazer, Sir James G. *The Golden Bough.* New York: Macmillan, 1922.

Gaster, Theodor. *Myth, Legend, and Custom in the Old Testament.* New York: Harper & Row, 1969.

Gifford, Edward S., Jr. *The Evil Eye.* New York: Macmillan, 1958.

Gilligan, Carol. *In a Different Voice.* Cambridge: Harvard University Press, 1982.

Gimbutas, Marija. *The Goddesses and Gods of Old Europe: Myths and Cult Images.* Berkeley and Los Angeles: University of California Press, 1974.

Goodrich, Norma Lorre. *Medieval Myths.* New York: New American Library, 1977.

Gornick, Vivian, and Barbara K. Moran, eds. *Woman in Sexist Society.* New York: New American Library, 1972.

Graves, Robert. *The Greek Myths.* 2 vols. New York: Penguin Books, 1955.

————. *The White Goddess.* New York: Vintage Books, 1958.

Greeley, Roger E. *The Best of Robert Ingersoll.* Buffalo: Prometheus Books, 1977.

Guerber, H. A. *Legends of the Middle Ages.* New York: American Book Co., 1924.

Haining, Peter. *Witchcraft and Black Magic.* New York: Grosset & Dunlap, 1972.

Hallet, Jean-Pierre. *Pygmy Kitabu.* New York: Random House, 1973.

Harding, M. Esther. *Woman's Mysteries, Ancient and Modern.* New York: Putnam, 1971.

Hartley, C. Gasquoine. *The Truth About Woman.* New York: Dodd, Mead, 1913.

Hartman, Mary, and Lois W. Banner, eds. *Clio's Consciousness Raised.* New York: Harper & Row, 1974.

Haskell, Molly. *From Reverence to Rape: The Treatment of Women in the Movies.* New York: Holt, Rinehart & Winston, 1974.

Hauswirth, Frieda. *Purdah: The Status of Indian Women.* New York: Vanguard Press, 1932.

Hazlitt, W. Carew. *Faiths and Folklore of the British Isles.* 2 vols. New York: Benjamin Blom, 1965.

Herodotus. *The Histories.* Translated by Henry Cary. New York: D. Appleton & Co., 1899.

Hobbs, Lisa. *Love and Liberation: Up Front With the Feminists.* New York: McGraw-Hill, 1970.

Hollander, Lee M. *The Skalds.* Ann Arbor: University of Michigan Press, 1968.

Hooke, S. H. *Middle Eastern Mythology.* Harmondsworth, U.K.: Penguin Books Ltd., 1963.

————. *The Siege Perilous.* Freeport, N.Y.: Books for Libraries Press, 1970.

Hyde, Walter Woodburn. *Greek Religion and Its Survivals.* New York: Cooper Square, 1963.

Janssen-Jurreit, Marielouise. *Sexism: The Male Monopoly on History and Thought.* New York: Farrar, Straus & Giroux, 1982.

Jonas, Hans. *The Gnostic Religion.* Boston: Beacon Press, 1963.

Joyce, P. W. *A Social History of Ancient Ireland.* 2 vols. New York: Arno Press, 1980.

Jung, C. G. *Psychology and Alchemy.* Princeton, N.J.: Princeton University Press, 1968.

Jung, Emma, and Marie-Louise von Franz. *The Grail Legend.* New York: Putnam, 1970.

Keightley, Thomas. *The World Guide to Gnomes, Fairies, Elves, and Other Little People.* New York: Avenel Books, 1978.

King, Francis. *Sexuality, Magic, and Perversion.* Secaucus, N.J.: Citadel Press, 1972.

Knight, Richard Payne. *The Symbolical Language of Ancient Art and Mythology.* New York: J. W. Bouton, 1892.

———. *A Discourse on the Worship of Priapus.* New York: University Books, 1974.

Kramer, Heinrich, and James Sprenger. *Malleus Maleficarum.* New York: Dover, 1971.

Larousse Encyclopedia of Mythology. London: Hamlyn Publishing Group Ltd., 1968.

Lea, Henry Charles. *The Inquisition of the Middle Ages.* New York: Citadel Press, 1954.

Lederer, Wolfgang. *The Fear of Women.* New York: Harcourt Brace Jovanovich, 1968.

Legge, Francis. *Forerunners and Rivals of Christianity.* 2 vols. New York: University Books, 1964.

Legman, G. *Rationale of the Dirty Joke.* New York: Grove Press, 1968.

Lethaby, W. R. *Architecture, Mysticism, and Myth.* New York: George Braziller, 1975.

Lindsay, Jack. *The Origins of Astrology.* New York: Barnes & Noble, 1971.

Loomis, Roger S., and Laura H. Loomis. *Medieval Romances.* New York: Modern Library, 1957.

Mahanirvanatantra. Translated by Sir John Woodroffe. New York: Dover, 1972.

Mâle, Emile. *The Gothic Image.* New York: Harper & Row, 1958.

Malory, Sir Thomas. *Le Morte d'Arthur.* 2 vols. London: J. M. Dent & Sons Ltd., 1961.

Malvern, Marjorie. *Venus in Sackcloth.* Carbondale: Southern Illinois University Press, 1975.

Massa, Aldo. *The Phoenicians.* Geneva: Editions Minerva, 1977.

Melamed, Elissa. *Mirror Mirror: The Terror of Not Being Young.* New York: Simon & Schuster, Linden Press, 1982.

Menen, Aubrey. *The Mystics.* New York: Dial Press, 1974.

Miles, Clement A. *Christmas Customs and Traditions.* New York: Dover, 1976.

Montagu, Ashley. *Sex, Man, and Society.* New York: Putnam, 1967.

Murstein, Bernard I. *Love, Sex, and Marriage Through the Ages.* New York: Springer Publishing Co., 1974.

Neumann, Erich. *The Great Mother: An Analysis of the Archetype.* Princeton, N.J.: Princeton University Press, 1963.

O'Flaherty, Wendy Doniger. *Hindu Myths.* Harmondsworth, U.K.: Penguin Books Ltd., 1975.

Pagels, Elaine. *The Gnostic Gospels.* New York: Random House, 1979.

Patai, Raphael. *The Hebrew Goddess.* Ktav Publishing House, 1967.

Pearsall, Ronald. *Night's Black Angels.* New York: McKay, 1975.

Pfeifer, Charles F. *The Dead Sea Scrolls and the Bible.* New York: Weathervane Books, 1969.

Phillips, Guy Ragland. *Brigantia: A Mysteriography.* London: Routledge & Kegan Paul, 1976.

Plaidy, Jean. *The Spanish Inquisition.* New York: Citadel Press, 1967.

Potter, Stephen, and Laurens Sargent. *Pedigree.* New York: Taplinger Publishing Co., 1974.

Pritchard, James B. *The Ancient Near East.* 2 vols. Princeton, N.J.: Princeton University Press, 1958.

Rank, Otto. *The Myth of the Birth of the Hero.* New York: Vintage Books, 1959.

Rawson, Philip. *Erotic Art of the East.* New York: Putnam, 1968.

———. *The Art of Tantra.* Greenwich, Conn.: New York Graphic Society, 1973.

Rees, Alwyn, and Brinley Rees. *Celtic Heritage.* New York: Grove Press, 1961.

Rich, Adrienne. *Of Woman Born: Motherhood as Experience and Institution.* New York: Norton, 1976.

Robbins, Rossell Hope. *Encyclopedia of Witchcraft and Demonology.* New York: Crown, 1959.

Robertson, J. M. *Pagan Christs.* New York: University Books, 1967.

Robinson, James M., ed. *The Nag Hammadi Library in English.* San Francisco: Harper & Row, 1977.

Ruether, Rosemary Radford. *Sexism and God-Talk: Toward a Feminist Theology.* Boston: Beacon Press, 1983.

Russell, J. B. *Witchcraft in the Middle Ages.* Ithaca, N.Y.: Cornell University Press, 1972.

Sadock, B. J., H. I. Kaplan, and A. M. Freedman, *The Sexual Experience.* Baltimore: Williams & Wilkins, 1976.

Scot, Reginald. *Discoverie of Witchcraft.* Yorkshire, U.K.: Rowmand & Littlefield, 1973.

Scott, George Ryley. *Phallic Worship.* Westport, Conn.: Associated Booksellers.

Seligmann, Kurt. *Magic, Supernaturalism, and Religion.* New York: Pantheon Books, 1948.

Shah, Idris. *The Sufis.* London: Octagon Press, 1964.

Shumaker, Wayne. *The Occult Sciences in the Renaissance.* Berkeley and Los Angeles: University of California Press, 1972.

Silberer, Herbert. *Hidden Symbolism of Alchemy and the Occult Arts.* New York: Dover, 1971.

Smith, Homer. *Man and His Gods.* Boston: Little, Brown, 1952.

Smith, John Holland. *The Death of Classical Paganism.* New York: Scribner, 1976.

Sobol, Donald J. *The Amazons of Greek Mythology.* Cranbury, N.J.: A. S. Barnes & Co., 1972.

Spence, Lewis. *An Encyclopedia of Occultism.* New York: University Books, 1960.

———. *The History and Origins of Druidism.* New York: Samuel Weiser Inc., 1971.

Squire, Charles. *Celtic Myth and Legend, Poetry and Romance.* New York: Bell Publishing Co., 1979

Steenstrup, Johannes C. H. R. *The Medieval Popular Ballad.* Seattle: University of Washington Press, 1968.

Stewart, Bob. *The Waters of the Gap.* Bath, U.K.: Pitman Press, 1981.

Stimpson, Catharine R., and Ethel Spector Person, eds. *Women: Sex and Sexuality.* Chicago: University of Chicago Press, 1980.

Stone, Merlin. *When God Was A Woman.* New York: Dial Press, 1976.

Sturluson, Snorri. *The Prose Edda.* Berkeley and Los Angeles: University of California Press, 1954.

Summers, Montague. *The Geography of Witchcraft.* New York: University Books, 1958.

Tatz, Mark, and Jody Kent. *Rebirth.* New York: Doubleday, Anchor Press, 1977.

Tennant, F. R. *The Sources of the Doctrines of the Fall and Original Sin.* New York: Schocken Books, 1968.

Trigg, Elwood B. *Gypsy Demons and Divinities.* Secaucus, N.J.: Citadel Press, 1973.

Tuchman, Barbara. *A Distant Mirror.* New York: Knopf, 1978.

Turville-Petre, E. O. G. *Myth and Religion of the North.* New York: Holt, Rinehart & Winston, 1964.

Vermaseren, Maarten J. *Cybele and Attis.* London: Thames & Hudson, 1977.

Waddell, L. Austine. *Tibetan Buddhism.* New York: Dover, 1972.

Wainwright, F. T. *Scandinavian England.* Sussex, U.K.: Phillimore & Co., Ltd., 1975.

Walker, Barbara G. *The Woman's Encyclopedia of Myths and Secrets.* San Francisco: Harper & Row, 1983.

Wedeck, Harry E. *A Treasury of Witchcraft.* Secaucus, N.J.: Citadel Press, 1975.

Wendt, Herbert. *It Began in Babel.* Boston: Houghton Mifflin, 1962.

Weston, Jessie L. *From Ritual to Romance.* New York: Peter Smith, 1941.

White, Andrew D. *A History of the Warfare of Science with Theology in Christendom.* 2 vols. New York: George Braziller, 1955.

Whitehouse, Ruth. *The First Cities.* New York: Dutton, 1977.

Wilkins, Eithne. *The Rose-Garden Game.* London: Victor Gallancz Ltd., 1969.

Wilson, Colin. *The Outsider.* Boston: Houghton Mifflin, 1956.

Wimberly, Lowry Charles. *Folklore in the English and Scottish Ballads.* New York: Dover, 1965.

Woods, William. *A History of the Devil.* New York: Putnam, 1974.

Zimmer, Heinrich. *Myths and Symbols in Indian Art and Civilization.* Princeton, N.J.: Princeton University Press, 1946.